Defi

Seven Life-Changing Lessons from Devastating Tragedy

JOHN RABINS

Illustrated by SARAH A. BOARDMAN

Edited by THOMAS WOMACK, BookOx

Firewall Press
Colorado Springs, Colorado

"One cannot grow lest he has been through the fire. May your new book bring hope and peace to the many who worship idols, or who feel they may be defined by *anything* other than God."

Carter Bradley Benedict, Cowboy Poet and Storyteller

Defined By Fire

Seven Life-Changing Lessons from Devastating Tragedy

Copyright © 2020 by  Firewall Press

ISBN (Paperback): 978-1-7345190-3-7

ISBN (ebook): 978-1-7345190-1-3

Dedication

*F*rom chapter 2 of this book: One morning I was doing my devotions and waiting for the Lord to speak to me. In the quiet of the moment, Obee, my Gordon Setter puppy, sneaked around from behind me and jumped on my lap. He laid his head on my shoulder against my face and let me love on him for what seemed a long time. He wanted nothing more than to be next to me. That was it—no expectations other than to be close to his "dad." He just wanted to be my kid. That's when God reminded me how that's exactly what He wants from me—that I just jump on His lap and into His arms so that He might console, comfort, encourage, and love me. Wow, what a revelation about the most important relationship in my life. The King of the universe wants to spend time with me!

Oil Portrait by Sarah A. Boardman

As crazy as this may seem, Defined by Fire is dedicated to Obee who taught me, better than any person or book could, what God's unconditional love really looks like.

Foreword

*T*his book throws a monkey wrench into what appears to be our current cultural values. What John writes here is a juxtaposition of what today's society says is genuinely important. Whether or not you're a follower of Christ, this book is for you. Why? Because we all need to be truth seekers. John shares, from his personal loss and tragedies, many profound truths which can be freeing for all of us. This book is a gut check on our priorities as humans. The following pages challenge what we value and how we see ourselves. At the end of each brief chapter, John raises penetrating questions which aren't easy to answer. His questions are unsettling to me! That's saying a lot, because in my profession as a strategic planning facilitator, my role is to ask challenging and stimulating questions.

Ten years ago, I met John in a wisdom sharing group composed of optometrists who were all seeking to improve their business management and practices. As the facilitator, I quickly determined that John was a "different cat," by no means your stereotypical OD. After retiring from a highly successful and decorated career as an avionics/aircraft maintenance officer, an Air Force Academy mathematics instructor, a physicist, and a unit commander (twice) in the United States Air Force, John went back to school to become an optometrist. John is humble, almost to the point of being embarrassed about the small-sized practice he established in Colorado Springs. This practice is different in a variety of ways.

First, although committed to improving his practice, John isn't the typical young, aggressive, financial data-driven OD. It quickly became apparent that John loves his employees and his patients, making decisions with the well-being of others as a critical factor in his thinking process.

Second, John provides vision care services to inmates at several prisons and jails in Colorado. Some optometric doctors—particularly if they have small practices—offer vision care in a prison only to supplement their income. But John does it because he cares about people.

Third, John doesn't have associate doctors or partners, preferring instead to own the entire practice.

But what really became clear to me and his fellow group members was that John makes decisions differently from most other doctors. He *prays* about significant decisions. Wait, man—this is a business, not a nonprofit or a church! But John doesn't compartmentalize; he brings his faith with him into the workplace.

If you are a Christ follower, this book will deepen your faith and hopefully realign your thinking. Few of us learn enough from major setbacks and tragedies. However, in *Defined by Fire*, John outlines seven powerful insights that he learned from losing everything. He helps us see ourselves and what we own through God's perspective of us and our possessions. John challenges the performance-based culture in which we seek to out-achieve the next guy. Oh, don't for a moment question John's degree of competitiveness. But his desire to excel is not to gain God's favor.

As believers, we want to honor God in all we do. However, we need to fully comprehend that God already accepts us exactly as we are. John hits a home run when he says: "The Christian life is not one of me becoming a better person—it's one of discovering the person God already sees me as."

Dick Schultz
Strategic Planning Facilitator, Tampa Bay, Florida

Defined By Fire

Seven Life-Changing Lessons from Devastating Tragedy

Contents

PART I

When the World Turns Upside Down

The Tragedy Unfolds

June 11, 2013:
A Day That Turned My Life Upside Down

The Spirit of the Sovereign Lord *is on me,*
because the Lord *has anointed me to preach good news to the poor.*
He has sent me to bind up the brokenhearted,
to proclaim freedom for the captives and release for the prisoners,
to proclaim the year of the Lord's *favor and the day of vengeance of our God,*
to comfort all who mourn, and provide for those who grieve in Zion—
to bestow on them a crown of beauty instead of ashes,
the oil of gladness instead of mourning,
and a garment of praise instead of a spirit of despair.
They will be called oaks of righteousness,
a planting of the Lord *for the display of His splendor.*
Isaiah 61:1-3

God took you to your knees, but His hand was out toward you,
beckoning you, the whole time."
Carter Bradley Benedict, cowboy poet and storyteller

This was a day I'll never forget.

I was in my optometry clinic seeing a patient when, within ten minutes, I received two earth-shaking telephone calls. The first informed me that the Black Forest (just north of Colorado Springs) was on fire, threatening and ultimately destroying my primary residence and rental around the corner. The second call was from my cousin Steve, who told me that my dad had just died.

Either of these pieces of news would shake me up to be sure. But both together had a terribly numbing effect—like, "This isn't really happening—I must be dreaming." But it wasn't a dream; the harsh reality of these tremendous losses became more graphic with each passing day. No home, no possessions, other than the few we were able to retrieve in the short time available to evacuate—and no earthly father. It was hard to wrap my arms around losses of this magnitude, particularly all at once.

Rarely does a day go by in which I don't think of something lost that simply cannot be replaced, such as the tiny eagle carved on the end of a matchstick that I purchased from a street artisan in Chile. I even lost the car I bought new as an Air Force Academy cadet, a 1972 Fiat 124 Spyder convertible.

It was as though all I have is God! A scary thought to be sure, but what a great place to be when we come to grips with what that truly means. As a Christian, I know intellectually that all I really need is Him. Frankly, as a good friend once reminded me, I don't even need air if I have Jesus; *everything* else pales in comparison.

I get that—intellectually. Translating that knowledge into practical living, my daily walk, has been a most difficult thing to do.

The day before I received those two calls—Monday, June 10—had been a hopeful day for me. I'd made flight arrangements to travel to Southern California on Wednesday the 12th to visit my eighty-six-year-old father, Buddy (as everyone called him; he disliked his given name, Bernard). I planned to help move my dad home from a rehab facility. I was excited to hear how well he was doing after nearly succumbing to kidney failure, heart disease, and a recalcitrant leg infection that seemed to take forever to heal.

But my exuberance was quickly quelled Tuesday morning when I learned that overnight my dad's systems began to shut down en masse, and he was back in emergency care. My mom called me early that morning in a panic; she was very afraid that after sixty-five years of marriage, she was losing her husband.

In spite of my attempts over the years to share the love of Christ with my parents, they never seemed to find the need for Him in their lives. So when my mom explained that she was losing her husband, she was truly frightened and handed the phone to Linda, the family caregiver. Linda knows the Lord and explained that my dad was about to die. She asked if I'd want to speak with him before his last breath.

"Can he talk?" I asked.

"No, he's in a coma," Linda replied, "but I know he'll hear you—hearing is the last sense to go. Here, John, I'm putting the phone to his ear; now say something!"

After uttering a quick prayer for divine wisdom, with tears streaming down my face, I said something like this: "Dad, this is your son, John. I hope you can hear me. I want you to know how much I love you. But I want you to know that there's someone who loves you far more than I do, and His name is Jesus. He's been knocking on the door of your life for a very long time, and He's standing at the door one last time before you enter eternity, beckoning you to allow Him in. I pray in Jesus' name that you'll do just that."

Those were the last words I spoke to my father. Wednesday's flight would now take me to a funeral instead of helping this hero of mine move back home.

On Tuesday, just after the fire began, my wife Nancy was stopped by a police barricade as she was returning from the veterinarian with our Gordon Setter puppy, Obee. Nancy turned the car around. After finding an alternate route to the house, she called me from the driveway. "I only have a few minutes," she exclaimed. "What shall I grab from the house?" We had a beautiful 6,500-square-foot home on five heavily forested acres. One would think that after the destructive Waldo Canyon fire to the west of us that damaged or destroyed over four hundred homes the previous year, we'd have created a list of items to grab should the same fate befall the Black Forest. Hard to imagine, but we had no such list, and we honestly believed the police barricade was just an exercise. Certainly we'd be returning to the house at some point in the near future.

We immediately thought of the following: the animals (two dogs, two cats, and our ball python, Shieka); the business and personal checkbooks; the business computer; and my radio-controlled watch. Nancy thought to grab my Bible, which had extensive notes from the past thirty years, and a quilt her mother had made. That was it, except for a basket of newly washed laundry. She was able to gather all the animals immediately, with the exception of Sam, our white cat, who was nowhere to be found. Sam was an expert at hiding, a veritable Houdini. This was *not* the time for her to play games. Nancy repeatedly called for her, to no avail. In desperation, Nancy screamed, "Sam, you have exactly *two* minutes to appear and save your life." Fortunately, Nancy found her soon thereafter.

She phoned me again from the driveway. "I have to get out of here; can you think of anything else I should retrieve?"

Without thinking I replied, "Well, I have to travel tomorrow. Could you go back in and get my toiletry bag?"

"Seriously? You really want me to go back in and get your toiletry bag?"

In a fleeting moment of sanity, I replied, "No. Get out of there—now!" Nancy and all the animals did just that.

The next day, Wednesday, found me sitting on the runway ready to depart for California. A three-word text from our renter around the corner indicated simply that "everything is gone." That included nine buildings on 11 acres—a hundred-year-old house, horse barn and stable, automotive repair shop, gunsmith shop, hay barn, a one-room church used by a holiness pastor in the late 1800s to early 1900s, some small cabins, and literally thousands of trees. Some historically important material things were gone in an instant.

Arriving Wednesday afternoon at my parents' gloomy house in California, I had lots of time to reflect. It was overwhelmingly difficult to grasp the magnitude of our tragedy. While praying late Wednesday afternoon before we knew whether our home was still standing, the Lord asked me to write down seven words, each beginning with the letters PR. Now, lest you misunderstand me, the Lord has rarely spoken to me in such a clear manner, but this to me was absolutely unmistakable as having come from Him. Some things you just know. The seven words revealed would be the steps Nancy and I would follow toward healing and restoration. The words were:

PROCESS
PRAY
PREPARE
PROVIDE
PROTECT
PREVAIL
PROSPER

They were, and still are, prophetic, as we watch God's providence unfold and His grace pour out before our very eyes.

Later, after learning of these special words, my friend Liz, a promotional products representative, created a keychain that I carry with me at all times (images below). One side has these seven words printed on it; the other shows a cross with this Scripture verse:

I can do all things through Christ who strengthens me. (Philippians 4:13, NKJV)

What's funny is that some time later, when I showed the keychain with all these "PR" words to one of my patients, she remarked how it was created by my "*promotional products professional.*" Of course this was probably sheer coincidence!

At this point in time our home had still not appeared on the official list of those destroyed. It was uncanny when my older son Michael texted me a link to a YouTube video (www.youtube.com/watch?v=up3kuTwBpsw) taken from a helicopter. The video (which I'm told went viral on the internet) showed our auxiliary garage and adjacent car in flames. My heart seemed to stop and I gasped as I observed our narrow driveway separating the destructive flames from our beautiful home. *That's my home,* I thought. *Is there any way, God, it might be spared?* By the end of the day we still didn't know if the house was standing.

The next day, Thursday, was my dad's funeral, and I was asked to speak publicly. About an hour before the service, I received a call from Nancy. "I know there's no good time to tell you this, babe, but we lost the house." I stood there dumbfounded for a time, trying to digest it all. It was certainly too much for me to process, but somehow at the service I managed to speak about my dad—noting his amazing generosity and likening it to the generosity of our heavenly Father, thus establishing my dad as an excellent role model during my formative years.

The next few days seemed to go by in slow motion: telephone conversations with the insurance companies; planning for my mom's future welfare; and wondering, praying, and planning, as best we were able, for our future. The seven "PR" words God had given me became very important to me just then, basically representing a roadmap for our recovery, an anchor of sorts. I found myself thinking about those words frequently throughout the day. I also found myself pondering my future as an optometrist, wondering whether it might be time to retire from the profession I truly loved.

I've commented at times that I don't go to work each day; I go to play. That makes sense when one considers that a third of my practice is children. What a joy!

Here are some joyous recollections of working with that particular population:

> A six-year-old girl, blonde and blue-eyed, was sitting in my exam chair and asked if I knew what the word *altitude* means.

I paused, wondering where she was going with this, then said, "Yes, of course. Do you know what it means?"

"It means height or elevation," she promptly replied.

Very impressive, I thought, then continued with her examination. She interrupted by asking if I knew what the word *plethora* means.

This floored me. I put my pen down and said, "I certainly *do* know what it means. It's a pretty big word—do *you* know what it means?"

"Yes," she quickly said, "it means 'a lot.'"

"Wow," I responded, "where are you learning words like that?" Remember, she was only six.

She placed her hands on her hips and proudly stated, "Well, I *am* in the first grade, you know!"

➤ I'm what you might call a behavioral (or functional) optometrist. That's one who believes that glasses aren't the only solution to vision problems, particularly focusing, binocular, or tracking problems. Sometimes vision therapy (VT), a regimen of eye exercises, represents a better approach.

An eleven-year-old girl named Kelly had just finished a twelve-week VT regimen and was about to say goodbye when she asked if I liked chocolate. I replied that indeed I did. She then asked if I liked white icing. Again I said of course I did.

Then she asked if I liked eyeballs.

"Why wouldn't I like eyeballs? I'm an eye doctor!"

She pulled from a bag a chocolate eyeball cake with white icing that she'd made for me. She even brought paper plates and utensils so she could serve slices to my staff and patients in the waiting room.

> It's a rare day that one doesn't hear laughter in our clinic. We love to tell old jokes and hear new ones. A little boy patient knew this and was excited to tell me one he'd just heard.

As he walked into my exam room, he tugged on my pant leg to get my attention, asking why the chicken crossed the playground. I confounded him by asking him why the chicken *didn't* cross the playground.

He had no idea. "Okay," he said, "why *didn't* the chicken cross the playground?"

"Because," I said, "he was *chicken!*"

Undaunted, he continued. "But why *did* the chicken cross the playground?" I had to admit I had no idea. He blurted out, "To get to the other *slide!*"

Despite these (and many more) delightful memories, I wondered if maybe I was losing the passion. When I shared with Nancy my thoughts about retiring, she quickly asked why I'd consider leaving the one semblance of normalcy in our lives. That was wisdom, making it much easier for me to decide to continue practicing, at least for the time being.

My good friend Dr. Rhonda Grigg, a pediatrician whom I'd accompanied on several medical mission trips to El Salvador, had been planning another trip in late October. She called me after the fire, telling me that she understood why I probably wanted to back out of the trip. "On the contrary," I told her. "I'm expecting to go with you, just as we've planned." What a good decision that turned out to be. Rhonda did pediatric care while Jamie, my technician who traveled with us, joined me in providing eye care for some of the poorest people on earth. In retrospect, I think the trip was more therapeutic for me than for the people we served.

The Lord worked mightily in my mind and heart through all this, literally dropping seven foundational truths in my lap that would ultimately serve as the basis for this book.

These truths have nothing to do with whether or not one is a Christian—they're true for everyone, regardless of belief. But they're fundamentally changing the way I think of myself in light of God's love for me and His definition of me as His child. They're changing the way I walk the Christian walk. There's neither mystery nor difficulty in these truths; after all, they come straight from the Scriptures.

So why has it taken me so long to truly begin to grasp them? Why did it take incredible tragedy to finally make me sit up and take notice?

I have no idea. But I do know this: tragedy will necessarily move you—either *toward* God, or *away* from Him.

There's no question He's finally getting my attention, and these truths are rocking my world from the inside out. May they revolutionize the way you view yourself and your role in God's kingdom. That's my sincere prayer for you.

> When you walk through the fire, you will not be burned; the flames will not set you ablaze. (Isaiah 43:2)

Additional Background – A Spiritual Upheaval

First Steps on the Exciting and Impossible Path of Faith

For you have been born again, not of perishable seed,
but of imperishable, through the living and enduring word of God.
1 PETER 1:23

Seek not greatness, but seek truth, and you will find both.
HORACE MANN, AMERICAN EDUCATOR

This chapter highlights several periods in my life that brought significant spiritual development—some life-changing moments in my search for truth. It is by no means meant to be exhaustive, only to give a sense of the exciting journey I'd been on prior to tragedy.

My Early Years

I was born into a Jewish family living in East Los Angeles. Well, we called ourselves Jewish, attended synagogue and Hebrew school, and celebrated the major holidays including the Sabbath each Friday night (though that tapered off as we grew older). But something was missing.

I was never sure just *what* we believed, though there was never a question that "Jews don't believe in Jesus"—that simple message was pounded home continuously. We called ourselves Conservative, but were actually Reform Jews at best. At thirteen I celebrated my bar mitzvah, and that was pretty much the end of my formal Jewish education.

We never read the Bible except to hear portions read in Hebrew during services. Hebrew is such a beautiful language to listen to, so it was a shame that my sister Karen and I never understood what was being read, except on the rare occasion when we looked at the translation. The synagogue service was simply a regular chore to be accomplished, and there was very little joy for us in doing it.

High School and College

My high school best friend, Matt, and I attended a Scientology meeting and ended up taking a sort of aptitude test. We went back a few times, but never really got into it. Even in high school I was searching for something. I just didn't know what it was.

I was fortunate to be recruited as a gymnast to the U.S. Air Force Academy. After being offered a recruiting slot, I was asked by the coach to compete for a congressional nomination, which I was able to do. While serving as a cadet, I continued my Jewish tradition by attending Jewish cadet services and singing in the Jewish choir. We were really quite awful, but had a marvelous time, particularly when we got to travel together.

During each of my four years at the Academy I participated on the rings for the varsity gymnastics team. We were very good, placing sixth in the NCAA championships our last two years.

On one road trip to Odessa, Texas, there was "nothing to do" after our meet. For entertainment, four of us went to a Southern Baptist revival meeting in a large church building. An evangelist named Richard Hogue spoke about everyone's need for Jesus and invited people to come down and make a profession of faith. I was so upset by his message that I told my friends I was going to "go down and straighten him out." They promised to wait for me in the foyer.

I went down all right and told him I was irritated with him. He asked if we might adjourn to a quieter place, to which I agreed, so we found another room in a different part of the building. He then asked me why I was upset. I quickly shared that many small children responded to his call of faith, some as young as three or four. "They couldn't possibly know what they were doing," I said, "and that bothers me."

He said it bothered him too, but he didn't know what he could do about it. He then asked if I had anything else on my mind that was bothersome.

His admission about the children had bolstered my confidence, so I proceeded to tell him that I had a problem with his idea of faith. After all, as a physics major at the U.S. Air Force Academy, I couldn't possibly have faith in something I couldn't see.

Pastor Hogue then took me along an amazing path, as it turned out. He began by simply asking if I'd ever been to Odessa before. I told him I hadn't. He then concluded that I'd never before been inside this building. Again I agreed. "What's that got to do with faith?" I asked.

What he said next was profound, though it didn't really hit me until later, after I had a chance to think about it. "While this isn't a perfect example," he said, "it seems to me you exercised faith when you entered this building—faith in the architect that he designed it properly, and faith in the builder that he built it according to specification, that it isn't just a hollow shell that could collapse and kill you." It took some time for me to realize that all my life I'd been exercising faith. When driving on a two-lane road, I have faith that the driver coming the other way will stay in his lane and not veer into mine. When boarding an airplane, I have faith that the pilot is competent to fly the plane. In fact, in today's world, I have faith that there even *is* a pilot, because rarely do I get to see him.

Pastor Hogue then said he thought I was very confused and that I probably shouldn't listen to him or anyone else who might be sharing the gospel with me.

"That doesn't make any sense," I replied. "Why would you ask me not to pay attention to what you just spent two hours speaking about?"

He asked if I'd ever read the Bible.

"Well, a little."

He challenged me to seriously read it. After I'd completed it, if nothing changed for me, then he suggested I go on living my life as before. I would at least have become familiar with the world's best-read book. But if God (who'd written that book as the pastor claimed) changed my life through it—would I be willing to follow after Him?

I was intrigued by this challenge. I told him I'd do it.

That night in my room, I prayed the first earnest prayer I'd ever truly offered. It was weak, but sincere. I looked up at the ceiling and said something like this: "God, I don't know who you are. Frankly, I don't even know *if* you are. But *if* you are, I'd like to know that—and I commit to reading this book that Pastor Hogue says comes from you. I won't listen to another person about all this until I've finished this book. *You* will have to be the one to convince me."

I'd pick up the Bible and read a little, then put it down. Pick it up, put it down. Again and again. It literally took me ten years to get serious about it, but serious I eventually became.

My Post-Academy Years

I met Becky during those cadet years, became smitten, and married her in the Jewish chapel just after graduation. She'd grown up in a Christian home but converted to Judaism so as not to upset my family, particularly my Grandma Zelda who considered herself an Orthodox Jew.

Seven years into the marriage, Becky and I separated and eventually divorced. An Air Force captain at the time, I found myself at Maxwell Air Force Base in Montgomery, Alabama in an eleven-week junior officer professional school. One thing

I remember most clearly about living in the humid South is the amazing number of cockroaches that greeted me on my return to the barracks for the evening. Actually, they quickly scattered, undoubtedly yelling something like, "Let's get outta here—he's home!" In the years since, I've thought long and hard about these hideous creatures, in light of evolution—a theory to which I once subscribed. Why was it, considering Darwin's survival-of-the-fittest doctrine, that these critters never "felt" they had to change? Just a thought, among many, that has bothered me for years regarding something formerly so dear to me.

Instead of studying as much as I should during this course of Air Force study at Maxwell AFB, I got very serious about the Bible and Christianity, knowing I needed something from outside myself, but still unsure how to get it. I knew deep down that the answer to my problems was something I couldn't generate on my own.

My best friend at this school, Vern, invited me to go to church with him, so I found myself attending Sunday services at Heritage Baptist Church in Montgomery. The senior pastor there, Andrew Smith, delivered consistently riveting messages. Frankly, I don't know how Vern and I passed the Air Force course, as we were up every night discussing my questions about the Bible. I seemed to have an insatiable appetite to know more, so I grilled Vern nonstop. He was patient with me, answering most of my questions outright. Those he wasn't confident about he would research and give me a good answer the next day.

I became an avid reader, picking up anything I thought might lead me to the answers I so desperately sought. I read the Bible cover to cover. Nothing earth-shattering happened yet, but I was certainly interested. I read a book by Bob Friedman entitled *What's a Nice Jewish Boy Like You Doing in the First Baptist Church?* I thought, *That was me.* Then I began reading *Mere Christianity* by C. S. Lewis, a book that intrigued me since Lewis presented the case for Christianity in an analytical fashion, something that resonated with my physics and mathematics background.

Halfway through the book, an incredible thing happened to me. Sitting on the edge of my bed one evening I noticed a personage sitting next to me. Now, I can't say that I could touch him as I might another human being, and I can't say that he looked like any other human being I'd met before, but there was no doubt he was as real to me then as any person has ever been. It was the Lord, and at that moment I absolutely *knew* that He was the Messiah I'd been reading about. Instantly I knelt before Him, confessed that I was a sinner needing salvation, and invited Him into my life.

This was the Saturday night before the last Sunday I'd attend Heritage prior to heading back to Colorado Springs. While excited beyond any expectation, I slept well that night, sensing a peace over me like never before.

The next morning I woke up and got ready to go to church with Vern. I didn't say anything about what happened the previous night. One thing they do very well in Baptist churches is regularly issue a call of faith, inviting anyone who wants to accept Jesus as Lord to come down to the front of the church. This shouldn't surprise us, as Jesus Himself called people publicly to affirm their faith in Him. Before the invitation was completed, I found myself at the altar (I think I must have run to it) waiting for what would happen next. As I looked to my right, there was Vern with tears in his eyes, placing his arm around me. It's what he'd been praying for consistently during the eleven-week course.

After the service, many came up and shook my hand, congratulating me on my decision. I felt so elated I could hardly contain myself. Many of these people, I learned, were encouraged by Vern to pray for me during the time I was in Montgomery. Who says there's no power in prayer? One of those who approached me congratulated me on becoming a "completed Jew." I didn't understand that term then, and I've never liked it since. The more I thought about it, the more I became convinced that in Christ there's no difference between a completed Jew and a completed Baptist. We all come to Him the same way—one on one. God really has *no* grandchildren. The apostle Paul tells us that "there is neither Jew nor Greek, slave nor free, male nor female, for you are all one in Christ Jesus" (Galatians 3:28).

A week after returning home to Colorado Springs, I received a telephone call from a man named John Upchurch, who told me he was the pastor of Heritage Baptist Church. On my exclaiming that he couldn't be, because Andrew Smith was the pastor of Heritage Baptist Church, he replied that these were two different churches having the same name but in two different cities. He said that Andrew and he were good friends and that Andrew had called, asking him to keep an eye on me. He then invited me to his church on Sunday.

I checked with Nancy, a fellow math instructor at the Air Force Academy, to see if she might be interested in coming along and, to my delight, she was. We attended together and simply loved it.

Nancy and I grew closer to each other as we grew closer to the Lord, and on August 31, 1980, we were baptized together in believers' baptism by Pastor Upchurch. Exactly one year later, on August 31, 1981, we were married by the same man.

And what an incredible journey it's been for us since then!

My Ph.D. Years—A Real Taste of the Journey

My perspective on the journey on which I was embarking was strengthened by a series of divine appointments during my Ph.D. program, in the mid-eighties at the University of New Mexico.

My advisor for my Lasers and Optical Physics track was Jim Small, Ph.D., a sensitive man who truly appreciated that he and I were of the same faith. He affectionately referred to me as "John the Evangelist," as I was quite vocal about my faith. I was so excited about the new life in me that I'd unreservedly talk to anyone about the Lord.

One day in study hall I found myself engaged with three or four fellow students in a spirited discussion about Christ. It felt like me against the world, since I was the only one supporting my position. The others disagreed strongly, attacking me (so I felt) from all sides. One of them was named Jim Roller, a loud, largish redhead who was downright abusive, in my view. During this ordeal I felt small and inadequate, but I continued to argue the faith as best I knew how. Afterward I was tired, feeling beat up and thinking I must have been ineffective at best.

God surely had His hand on me during this time. I'd begun the Ph.D. program after these other students, but finished my course work before they did, and was off to do my dissertation long before they were. My dissertation was an experimental one that I prepared in one of the labs at the Air Force Weapons Laboratory on Kirtland AFB, New Mexico. One morning, out of the blue, came a call from someone who said he wanted to meet with me—it was Jim Roller. I thought, *What do you want now, to verbally abuse me some more?* On the phone, however, he was soft-spoken and polite. "Certainly," I told him, "Why don't you come by the lab this afternoon?"

That afternoon there was a knock on the door. I must admit that I still felt a bit uneasy. Jim followed me to the office at the back of the lab and sat down next to me. His countenance was different from the man I'd remembered: his head was lowered, and he appeared sad. He shared that his wife told him that morning that she was pregnant and wanted a divorce. He cried as he shared this with me, stating that he knew he needed Jesus in his life. "Would you help me with that?" he asked.

"Certainly," I told him, then led him in a simple prayer during which he invited Jesus into his life.

I was privileged to see Jim a few times after that historic meeting, happily finding him joyfully pursuing the path of faith. I've long since lost touch with him, but I know he willingly placed his life into God's hands, and I'm comforted by that knowledge.

I stopped sharing my faith at one point during my Ph.D. program, not because I was embarrassed or losing my faith, but because I'd been reflecting on the importance of the words coming out of my mouth. With the wrong selection of words, I might drive someone away from Christ as opposed to drawing them toward Him. So I became very quiet, not sharing anything with anyone. My advisor noticed this. He called me into his office and asked why I'd become so quiet.

"I guess I just don't want to offend anyone with the wrong words," I responded, "so I've taken a safe road for now."

I'll never forget what happened next. Jim laid into me, asking just who I thought I was, after all! "John, you've blown your role as Christ's ambassador completely out of proportion! Look at it this way: Jesus is the fisherman, the Holy Spirit is the hook, and you're only the worm, just a piece of bait. Your sole job is to wiggle around a bit and attract attention." That took a lot of pressure off me, and I've reflected on the wisdom of that message many times since.

Another divine encounter was with Juice (our affectionate nickname for him), a special guy I met in one of my classes. He was a young Air Force officer, and we hit it off immediately. I knew he was different from most of our classmates. It turned out he was a new Christian, and we spent many days after class discussing various elements of the faith.

One day after our discussion, he asked if I'd pray for him, as he was struggling with something. He never shared exactly what it was. I placed my hand on his shoulder and prayed for him. I was surprised to find myself speaking in tongues, something I'd not done before but was aware of from my New Testament readings. I honestly had no idea about that which I was praying, but I learned the following week that it must have been very important.

I invited Juice to come to our house for a barbeque the upcoming weekend. When the time came, Nancy and I were excited, had the hamburgers and fixings all ready, and started the charcoals. But Juice never showed up. *The nerve,* I thought. He didn't even call to apologize or answer his phone when I tried to call him. I planned to confront him the next week during class, but he didn't show up for class Monday, Tuesday, Wednesday, or Thursday. I began to worry about him.

Then the following article appeared in the obituary section of the Albuquerque Tribune on Friday, February 25, 1983:

KAFB Engineer Dies When Electrocuted

An Air Force electrical engineer was killed while working with high-voltage equipment at the Air Force Weapons Laboratory at Kirtland Air Force Base. Second Lt. Guice B. Vander Linden, 23, of Honolulu, Hawaii, was electrocuted at 11:05 a.m. Thursday, said Lt. Phil Hutchison of the Weapons Lab. He said medical teams were called to the scene immediately but could not save Vander Linden. He was pronounced dead about an hour later at Lovelace Medical Center after unsuccessful resuscitation attempts at the laser laboratory and Lovelace, a Lovelace spokesperson said. Vander Linden worked in the Advanced Laser technology Division at Kirtland. He resided at 3320 Wyoming Blvd. N.E. He was single and has relatives in Hawaii. Hutchison said Air Force officials are investigating the specific cause of Thursday's accident.

This had a profound impact on me and made me realize that as Christians, our "chance" meetings are not accidental. In fact, I believe our sovereign God orchestrates so much of which we're simply unaware. We're called to walk by faith, believing that He truly is in control. That certainly takes a lot of pressure off of us.

Do I have doubts and questions about my faith at times? Of course I do! But this one thing I know with absolute certainty: the Christian walk is an exciting one and, while no two Christians are on the exact same path, we're all heading in the exact same direction toward the exact same goal. It's comforting to know that God really is in control; He loves us with an unshakable, unconditional love, and He'll never release us from His hand!

PART II

The Seven
Defining Truths

*Then you will know the truth
and the truth will set you free.*
JOHN 8:32

You'll recall that God gave me those seven **"PR"** words to chart the course through devastating tragedy toward healing and victory. Here they are, once again:

PROCESS
PRAY
PREPARE
PROVIDE
PROTECT
PREVAIL
PROSPER

God also dropped in my lap the seven defining truths that comprise the remainder of this book. That there are seven is no surprise, since the number seven is commonly used— seven wonders of the world, seven deadly sins, seven seas, seventh heaven, Snow White and the Seven Dwarfs—you get my drift. We find the number seven throughout both biblical and secular literature, such as Napoleon Hill's seven positive emotions and seven negative emotions in his classic book *Think and Grow Rich*. One may do a fairly exhaustive internet search to discover literally page upon page upon page of references to the number seven, both inside and outside Scripture. While unimportant, it's interesting that it took seven years from the tragedy to the printing of this book.

Believe me, I get it—seven is an important number! So it came as no surprise, following our tragedy, that each list God has given me contains seven elements.

The seven defining truths that make up the following seven chapters have literally shaken my thinking. On the surface, they seem quite obvious and believable to even the most casual Christian, even perhaps to some who don't espouse Christianity. But these truths will absolutely move you if you dwell on them for any length of time. They'll transform your thinking and your life, if you let them.

Here they are:

1. I am not defined by what I own; rather, I'm defined by Him who owns me.

2. I am not defined by what I've done; rather, I'm defined by what He has done.

3. I am not defined by my tragedies and dark places; rather, I'm defined by Him who carries me through tragedy and is the Light in my dark places.

4. I am not defined by what I think; rather, I'm defined by what He thinks.

5. I am not defined by what you think (or anyone else, for that matter); rather, I'm defined by what He thinks.

6. I am not defined by what I control; rather, I'm defined by Him who controls everything.

7. I am not defined by who I know; rather, I'm defined by Him who knows me best.

I recently read a compelling newspaper article about Dan Oosterhous, the courageous coach of the Air Force Academy men's tennis team. Dan was an accomplished athlete when he was a cadet in the early nineties, playing tennis at number one singles. His fifty-six victories rank fifth on Air Force's all-time career list, and as a senior he went 22-3, the fourth-best season record for a number one player in program history. He became tennis coach in 2009—then suffered two major strokes in early 2013, which rendered him paralyzed on one side.

Dan gets what defines him. "There's nothing to be upset about," he said. "This is nobody's fault. It's not my fault; it could have happened to anybody. It happened to me, so what am I going to do about it? I can choose to be bitter, or I can try to get better. So that's what I'm going to do." He adds, "My strokes will be a permanent part of my life, but *they won't define me."*

So what defines you?

At the end of each of the following seven chapters, you'll find personal application questions. In defining myself, it took the devastating loss of home and personal property to help me begin understanding how my earthly relationships and possessions pale in comparison to my relationship with God. How might I convey even a portion of that understanding to someone who hasn't been through a similar experience? How could I create a vicarious experience for someone who hasn't seen it firsthand? Good questions, you'll likely agree— and they're precisely my goal as I pose thought-provoking application questions at the end of each of the chapters to come. They're designed to be explored in group discussion where others can share from their life experiences, although I believe there's also benefit in pondering them alone, in private study.

Note that many of these questions are intentionally difficult—*they're meant to challenge.* Some of them may be uncomfortable for you to think about, let alone discuss with others. You may find some too emotionally charged to consider right now, or perhaps your group isn't a good fit for discussing some of them. That's perfectly fine; leave those for now and come back to them later. Some questions may need to be readdressed multiple times over time. If you *are* uncomfortable with some of them, may I suggest that perhaps God has some work yet to do in your life? To obtain the most meaningful results, do your best to steer clear of any pat, textbook answers; rather, allow your heart to speak more and your head less. Remember, the questions are intentionally open-ended, without any "right" or "wrong" answers.

So let's get your "shovels" ready as we dig in and begin to unpack these seven important truths. My sincere hope is that God will use these chapters and their application questions to challenge you to go deeper with Him than you ever thought possible. May your walk with Him become richer, and the grace you share with others sweeter.

What I Own

Then he said to them, "Watch out! Be on your guard
against all kinds of greed; a man's life does not consist
in the abundance of his possessions." And he told them this parable:
"The ground of a certain rich man produced a good crop.
He thought to himself, 'What shall I do? I have
no place to store my crops.'
Then he said, 'This is what I'll do. I will tear down my
barns and build bigger ones,
and there I will store all my grain and my goods. And I'll say to myself,
"You have plenty of good things laid up for many years.
Take life easy; eat, drink and be merry."'
But God said to him, 'You fool!
This very night your life will be demanded from you.
Then who will get what you have prepared for yourself?'
This is how it will be with anyone who stores up things for himself
but is not rich toward God."
LUKE 12:15-21

Do not store up for yourselves treasures on earth,
where moth and rust destroy,
and where thieves break in and steal. But store
up for yourselves treasures in heaven,
where moth and rust do not destroy, and where thieves
do not break in and steal.
For where your treasure is, there your heart will be also.
MATTHEW 6:19-21

There's a popular old saying: he who dies with the most toys wins. There's another saying: you can't take it with you. And let's add one more: eat, drink, and be merry, for tomorrow we die.

Unfortunately there's a flagrant, fatal flaw with each of these ways of thinking. Each places far more importance on this life than the life to come. It's as though nothing else matters outside our existence on earth. How short-sighted that is! But that's exactly what I used to think. The more I accumulated, the more "secure" I became.

And accumulate we did: thousands of professional books and cookbooks, dozens of boxes filled with items, boxes that moved from one Air Force station to another without being opened (I couldn't even tell you what was in most of them), and hundreds of pictures, trinkets, and other collectibles one just "cannot do without." I certainly don't mean to minimize the sentimental value of material things, but I now see more clearly the unhealthy, misplaced value I once placed on things, as well as titles, career choices, pets, and even relationships.

An interesting observation that Nancy once shared with me involved a survey conducted in which people were asked how much more money they'd need to earn in order to feel "comfortable." An amazing insight from the survey emerged: no matter how much people were currently making, whether it be $10,000 a year or $10 million a year, the answer they gave was almost always the same: "about a third more." Isn't that fascinating and ironic at the same time? No one seems happy with what they have; they "need" a third more for that to happen. By deductive reasoning, when you think about it, *no one will ever be content.*

Here's what I'm learning through tragic loss:

**I am not defined by what I own;
rather, I'm defined by Him who owns me.**

Besides the unique items lost that cannot be replaced, I really haven't missed very much. In fact, I'd be hard-pressed to even recall what most of it was. One of my biggest anxiety-provoking concerns over the past few years was how I was eventually going to get rid of most of the clutter so it wouldn't become a problem for my children. And while I wouldn't wish a tragedy of this magnitude to happen to anyone else, Nancy and I both say unequivocally that a fire can be an incredibly efficient decluttering tool! Not to mention a magnificent sense of freedom that simply cannot be ignored.

Don't Die with New T-Shirts!

I love new things. In fact, I've attached an unreasonable value to new things *just* because they're new. Here's the problem with that thinking: by using something even once, it's no longer new, and thus not as valuable. I know it sounds crazy, but that's exactly how I once thought, and still do if I'm not on my guard.

As an example of what I'm convinced must be some sort of mental illness, I've owned hundreds of new T-shirts: beautiful animal prints, Hard Rock Café shirts, college and university shirts, and a myriad of other varieties. I collected them from all over the world. I loved them so much that I'd fold them uniformly and neatly, then store them on shelves and in drawers (let's not forget that I'm prior military). Periodically I'd look at those shirts and remind myself how fortunate I was to own them. I'd find myself whispering something like this: "Wow, that one's *so* beautiful; one day I'll be sure to wear it." But the sad fact is that I never did, and consequently lost hundreds of new T-shirts in a fire.

God spoke clearly to me through all this: "John, if I gift you, whether with something tangible, as a T-shirt, or with a spiritual gift, you're to *use* it. Otherwise, you risk losing it." What a powerful message that is! Since then, every new T-shirt and every new pair of shoes, with few exceptions, I've worn. My new (to me) sports car, which replaced my old cadet sports car that was damaged almost beyond recognition, gets driven nearly every week, though part of me would rather keep it new. I'm learning to appreciate even those things that are used. They're becoming special to me in a very different way.

Some Unlikely Valuables That "Survived" the Fire

My neighbor Bill assumed responsibility for organizing the effort of sifting through the ashes at our destroyed house. There were many who helped—neighbors, volunteers from a local Air Force Base, church members, and patients. Some showed up whom I didn't know at all. It was truly humbling to see the outpouring of love they showed our family. Bill would allow neither Nancy nor me to sift; rather, he insisted that others sift and bring to us things we might find valuable.

In spite of the fact that people were genuinely excited to show us "treasures" they retrieved, most of the finds, unfortunately, were pretty much beyond recognition and consequently worthless. One sifter brought me an inscribed metal silver plate in the shape of a shield that was badly gnarled and burnt; in fact, it had turned dark shades of black and yellow. The sifter excitedly asked me what it was. Only a few words were visible, but I soon recognized my Academy diploma. The wood backing, of course, was no longer attached. I remember staring at it in disbelief for a while before announcing what it was.

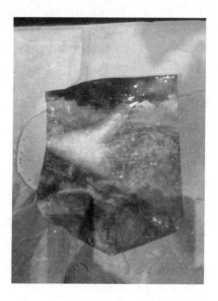

I decided to keep it, along with my old Academy dog tags, plus my cadet car's gas cap, original keys, and a hub cap, and some other of my cadet possessions. I've created a shadow box with these items in it, along with some before-and-after pictures. On the top, an inscriptive plaque of moss rock that burned and fell off the house is etched with these words:

THROUGH THE "FIRE"—1969-1973
AND ONCE AGAIN—JUNE 11, 2013

It now hangs in my study, where I can see it every day.

A special friend once challenged me to consider the following:

"One's anxiety comes from wanting a future outcome over which he has no control. *What do you need to let go of in order to live in the present, with joyfulness, John?*" she asked me. After praying about this, the Lord gave me, not surprisingly, *seven* things, each corresponding to one of the *seven* definitional truths, and each capping a definitional chapter. They are underlined to clearly identify them. Here's the one relating to possessions:

What I Need to Let Go of:

The Fear That Joy is Somehow Outside My Reach

Webster defines *joy* as "the emotion evoked by well-being, success, or good fortune or by the prospect of possessing what one desires," or as "the state of happiness or felicity." By this definition, certainly lots of things can bring us joy—our household possessions, our automobiles, our real estate, our pets, our relationships, our favorite football team, our career or job.

But I think there's a big difference between "joy" and "happiness." I used to think the two words meant exactly the same thing. That's in part why I'd collected so many possessions, including all those T-shirts. The more I had, I figured, the happier I'd be. Instead, I discovered that having more stuff only led to the desire for more stuff, not necessarily more happiness. In fact, I was pretty miserable at times while I was planning to acquire more of something.

I no longer feel this way. Happiness and joy are two entirely different concepts. To me, happiness has a temporal aspect to it, while joy has a more eternal perspective.

A dictionary definition of *happiness* is "a state of well-being, a pleasurable or satisfying experience." The definition of the word *rejoice* (related to our word *joy*) is "to feel great delight, to welcome or to be glad." It's interesting that the Bible uses the words "happy" and "happiness" 30 times, while "joy" and "rejoice" appear over 300 times. But there's no better definition of joy than one by Rick Warren that's quoted in Kay Warren's book, *Choose Joy: Because Happiness Isn't Enough.* Here's what Rick says:

> Finding joy is a challenge for me. I'm not naturally an upbeat person; I'm more of a melancholy. When I talk about joy, I'm not doing so from the perspective of a generally peppy person who never has a bad day. In fact, it's because of my own inability to live with joy that led me to explore why my experiences didn't line up with Scripture.

> My problem was my definition of joy. I thought joy meant feeling good all the time. That's impossible! Even for those who are naturally upbeat and optimistic, that's impossible. We have to start somewhere more realistic—and closer to Scripture.

So here's the definition I've come up with from studying Scripture: *Joy is the settled assurance that God is in control of all the details of my life, the quiet confidence that ultimately everything is going to be alright, and the determined choice to praise God in every situation.*

You'll find nothing in that definition about happy feelings, because, as we all know, happiness is fleeting and temporary.

We tend to think that life comes in hills and valleys. In reality, it's much more like train tracks. Every day of your life, wonderful, good things happen that bring pleasure and contentment and beauty to you. At the exact same time, painful things happen to you or those you love that disappoint you, hurt you, and fill you with sorrow. These two tracks—both joy and sorrow—run parallel to each other every single moment of your life.

That's why, when you're in the midst of an amazing experience, you have a nagging realization that it's not perfect. And while you're experiencing something painful, there's the glorious realization that there is still beauty and loveliness to be found. They're inseparable.

If you look down train tracks into the brightness of the horizon, the tracks become one. You can't distinguish them as two separate tracks. That's how it will be for us, too. One day, our parallel tracks of joy and sorrow will merge into one. The day we meet Jesus Christ in person and see the brightness of who He is, it will all come together for us. Then it will all make complete sense.

I like that—a lot! I certainly couldn't say it any better, and I often ponder the illustration.

There's No Greater Possession Than Jesus

No question, it's nice to own things. Things make our lives both easier and more pleasurable, and God is certainly not opposed to our owning them. But we must remember that they're not really ours to keep. We come into the world with nothing, and we leave with nothing. While things are nice to have and use, they're not necessary.

I mentioned earlier my friend's statement that even air isn't necessary if you've got Jesus. How true that is! To the degree we rely on things instead of the Lord, we're missing something, I think.

Application Questions about Possessions

1. Of all your physical possessions, which one would you be most bothered to permanently lose or have stolen from you? It might be a special car, a unique collectible, a gift, or something else. Why do you feel so attached to it?

2. Think about that special physical possession again. Imagine that it was permanently lost or destroyed in a fire or other disaster. What will you do now, knowing it will never return? Now that it's gone, has your opinion about God or your relationship with Him changed? How? And why?

3. Outside of your relationship with God, what earthly relationship do you value the most? In other words, if you could hang on to only one earthly relationship, which would it be? What is your second most important relationship? And third?

4. Imagine coming home after a long day to find that your home has been broken into and ransacked, and the

person who is your second most important relationship is lying on the floor of the living room, having been brutally murdered. What are your immediate thoughts or emotions? Beside police and emergency services, who will you call first? What is your initial plan of action?

5. Now imagine that a full year goes by with neither closure nor even a clue regarding the identity of the murderer. How has your thinking changed? How about your relationship with God? What's your plan of action now? Is your approach different from before?

6. Have you ever wondered who you really belong to? Have you asked yourself who or what has control over you? What did you conclude?

7. If someone bought a lottery ticket for you, and you won five million dollars—what would you do with all that money?

What I've Done

*Therefore, there is now no condemnation for
those who are in Christ Jesus,
because through Christ Jesus the law of the
Spirit of life set me free
from the law of sin and death.*
ROMANS 8:1-2

*Therefore, if anyone is in Christ, he is a new creation;
the old has gone, the new has come!*
2 CORINTHIANS 5:17

*For it is by grace you have been saved, through
faith—and this not from yourselves,
it is the gift of God—not by works, so that no one can boast.
For we are God's workmanship, created in Christ
Jesus to do good works,
which God prepared in advance for us to do.*
EPHESIANS 2:9-10

I've always been performance-oriented. While I'm not quite sure how that happened, here's what it looks like practically: *to be loved and accepted, I must perform, and perform well.*

Certainly my family never expressed that to me in words when I was growing up. They were very supportive of everything I did—academics, gymnastics, musical pursuits, debate club, etc. In fact, they never missed a gymnastics meet, always in the grandstands rooting me on. They showed up for my piano recitals. They were at all my school academic award ceremonies. That included my dad's mom, Grandma Mary. Even now I vividly remember her proud smile and encouragement. It was great knowing they were there for me.

Nevertheless, I somehow got the idea that to be worthy of love, I had to perform. And perform I did! I worked hard in everything I attempted, earning distinctions and awards in academics, sports, and music—you name it. Growing up, I had trophies all over my bedroom and medals hanging from my high school letterman sweater. There were plaques on the wall and achievements galore.

I even achieved the rank of colonel during my twenty-five-year Air Force career. My Air Force uniforms bore many medals. Many of these were packed away in boxes in our Colorado home. I'm not sure exactly what I planned to do with them, but it was nice occasionally to think about their being there—somewhere.

They're not there anymore; all were consumed in the fire. Not a single physical reminder of those achievements exists today, except the one I mentioned—the charred remains of my Academy diploma dug up from the ashes.

What's interesting is that I don't think much these days about those achievements. It's not that the accomplishments were unimportant, or that human successes aren't worth pursuing. It's simply this:

> **I am not defined by what I've done;
> rather, I'm defined by what He has done.**

This very important fact should take a lot of pressure off me. But I'm discovering that I'm on a journey, and by no means have arrived in this area. While I've made some progress, it's so easy to forget that it's *not* about performance, and I find myself dropping my guard sometimes and reverting to the performance mode for acceptance and love. Old habits, it seems, are hard to break.

Having It Made

I once thought that on reaching high school I would have "arrived." I quickly found out that a high school freshman is anything *but* a success. I needed to get past my freshman year to be the success I dearly desired to be. Then I discovered that sophomores and juniors had nothing on seniors, so I'd have to wait till my senior year to see what success really looked like. It felt good to be a senior, I must admit. Doing well in academics and gymnastics had its associated perks, including being the school mascot who dressed up as Joe Aztec and tumbled out on the football field with the cheerleaders.

A funny thing happened after graduation, though. I became a freshman—or doolie, or squat—at the Air Force Academy, the lowest of the low. It was like I was starting all over again. Actually, it was worse. I remember sitting at the dining table for our last dinner of the three-day orientation, the very last meal before basic cadet training (BCT) would officially begin. As we were looking around Mitchell Hall, the 4,000-seat dining facility we'd come to know well, our assigned senior at the head of the table told us to take a good look around. We were puzzled, especially when he told us to take a good hard look at the ceiling, because we wouldn't see it again for a year. From the beginning of BCT until hell week was over, we weren't allowed to gaze around, but only keep our eyes caged downward in front of us unless we were addressed by an upperclassman or an officer. And then we were allowed only one of four responses—"yes, sir," "no, sir," "no excuse, sir," or "sir, may I ask a question?" Everywhere we walked—outside or in the dining hall,—our eyes were caged. Humiliating to be sure.

Hell Week would certainly mark the end of our feeling less than human, we reasoned. But it didn't. We were still doolies, albeit with extra privileges. We'd have to wait to become third classmen (sophomores) in order to feel as though we'd arrived, since then we'd officially be upperclassmen.

But wait—first we had to go through SERE (Survival, Escape, Resistance, and Evasion), a three-week program where we were treated as POWs. Not fun at all. But after *that* we would indeed be real upperclassmen.

I'm hoping you see a pattern here. Becoming a third classman, even after successfully finishing SERE, was no picnic. Neither was being a second classman (junior). Even first classmen were nothing compared to commissioned officers, so we'd have to wait until graduation to finally *arrive*. But the pattern continued, and I learned after graduation that second lieutenants were lower than the low, and it started all over again.

We *never* arrive! No one ever has, no one ever will. So the real question is why we try so hard to arrive when in fact we never do.

The answer's simple, really: we don't see ourselves as human "beings," but as human "doings."

What I Need to Let Go of:

Viewing Myself as a Human "Doing" Versus a Human "Being"

Now, it's not fair to leave you with the impression that I've excelled at everything I've ever attempted. Certainly it could have looked that way on the outside to the casual observer. But there have been failures in my performance; you'll recall that I've been divorced, as a prime example, and I wouldn't consider for a moment blaming it on anyone else.

The point I want to make is that God loves me not because of what I've done, but because of what He has done—it's His very nature. This fact is one of the hardest for me to accept and appropriate into my daily living. But day by day, it's beginning to become clearer. Here's a guy who always thought that his *performance* earned love, and here's a God who says He loves me *unconditionally*. Obviously, those are two mutually exclusive ideas; they cannot both be true. If I'm to believe what God says, that means it doesn't matter what I've done or what I do—He will still love me. How can that be? As fallen human beings, that's a difficult concept to grasp, but it's what He says. The thief on the cross beside Jesus discovered that beautiful truth as he was about to take his last breath (read about it in Luke 23:39-43).

If we were to introspectively evaluate how much of us comprises "doing" vs "being," I fear the former part would be deemed by most of us to be far more important than the latter. That's unfortunate, but that seems to be what our culture values. It's sad because it's not the part God values. Sometimes I think that our "doing" just hampers what God wants to do in our life and (through us) in others' lives. More and more, when I'm tempted to ask God what I can do for Him today, I'm reminded how that must disappoint Him. He probably just shakes His head, thinking, *What do you mean—what can YOU do for Me today? Just appreciate everything I've done for you, and be My kid!.*

I'm becoming convinced that God wants me to just *be*—be His kid, be His beloved, be the apple of His eye. A friend from church once remarked, "There's nothing you can do to please God except know that you're walking in His grace." I think that sums it up quite nicely.

One morning I was doing my devotions and waiting for the Lord to speak to me. In the quiet of the moment, Obee, my Gordon Setter puppy, sneaked around from behind me and jumped on my lap. He laid his head on my shoulder against my face and let me love on him for what seemed a long time. He wanted nothing more than to be next to me. That was it—no expectations other than to be close to his "dad." He just wanted to be my kid. That's when God reminded me how that's exactly what He wants from me—that I just jump on His lap and into His arms so that He might console, comfort, encourage, and love me. Wow, what a revelation about the most important relationship in my life. The King of the universe wants to spend time with me!

Obee (right) and his best buddy, Aries

My counselor once asked me, "What do you have to *do*, John -- in order to *be*?" Good question, and my counselor refused to answer just then, desiring that I spend a good deal of time pondering it. Months later, he finally gave me the answer. He said it's found in the Psalms, especially this verse:

Be still and know that I am God. (Psalm 46:10)

Could it really be that simple? I'm slowly learning that the answer to that is a resounding -- *be still and know!* All my doings are pretty much meaningless—unless, of course, they arise from my being. I need to work on *doing* less and *being* more!

There's a powerful book called *The Cure* (by John Lynch, Bruce McNicol, and Bill Thrall) that includes this bold statement: "On my worst day, God cannot love me any more and He will not love me any less." Wow! Think about your worst day ever and apply that kind of thinking. Not easy, is it? But God said it, so it must be true.

My own worst day ever occurred during my Air Force years, a day when willful sin took hold of me in a big way. I was in huge rebellion, and I remember shaking my fist toward heaven, challenging God: "Forgive that, I dare you!" I believed there was no way He could. The incredible thing is that He did!

Christ's sacrifice on the cross was big enough to cover all my sin—past, present, and future. I rarely doubt that any more.

Application Questions about Performance

1. List some of the successes you've experienced in your life, from childhood onward; there are likely many you can recall. Which accomplishments are you most proud of? Why do you feel that way?

2. Have you ever found yourself thinking that once you met a certain milestone, you'd have it made? Is it true that we *never* really "arrive"? Why or why not?

3. Do you serve in God's kingdom from a performance-based mentality or from a heart that worships Him? How do we move from the former to the latter? What must you *do* in order to *be*?

4. Does God love you more when you're doing His will than when you're walking in disobedience? Why do we find it hard to believe that God's love for us doesn't depend on what we do? How can God truly love us when we're walking in disobedience? Do you really believe that to be true?

5. Have you ever had a dog that loved you unconditionally? What was it like being together? Why is it so easy for a dog to do that, but so difficult for us as humans?

6. Do talented and successful people have a harder time understanding the unconditional love of God than those not as talented or successful? Why or why not?

7. Recount a situation in which someone showed you unconditional love. Could you do that for someone else? Have you?

My Tragedies

God is our refuge and strength, an ever present help in trouble.
Therefore we will not fear, though the earth give way
and the mountains fall into the heart of the sea,
though its waters roar and foam
and the mountains quake with their surging.
Psalm 46:1-3

I have told you these things, so that in me you may have peace.
In this world you will have trouble. But take heart!
I have overcome the world.
John 16:33

The Lord *is close to the brokenhearted and*
saves those who are crushed in spirit.
A righteous man may have many troubles, but the
Lord *delivers him from them all;*
he protects all his bones, not one of them will be broken.
Psalm 34:18-19

In some weird way, most people seem to enjoy talking about tragedy, especially if it's their own. There's something comforting about others showing interest and sympathy in your personal misfortune; indeed, it makes you feel important.

I actually got caught up into this kind of thinking following the fire, and I've since been fascinated with this sort of mentality. Some people seem not to be happy unless they're miserable, and they tend to gather around them those who are equally miserable—to commiserate (*co-miserate*—to "miserate" together). Their tragedy or misfortune can become a badge of honor of a sort.

This thinking represents the height of a victim mentality. Novelist Tom Robbins has aptly said, "The unhappy person resents it when you try to cheer him up, because that means he has to stop dwelling on himself and start paying attention to the universe. Unhappiness is the ultimate form of self-indulgence."

This type of behavior and thinking seems most futile to me as I learn this truth:

I am not defined by my tragedies and dark places; rather, I'm defined by Him who carries me through tragedy and is the Light in my dark places.

It's been said that 95 percent of the world entertains a victim mentality, which leaves only 5 percent with a victor mentality. Why is that? Beats me.

But I do know this—the 5 percent are out there, and they're worth seeking out.

One of the 5 percent that Nancy and I were privileged to work alongside years ago was Jim Rewalt, a fellow instructor in the Air Force Academy mathematics department. Jim and his wife Cille (short for Lucille) have surely had their share of loss and heartbreak. Their six-year-old daughter Jenny was struck by a car in 1981 while on the bicycle she'd just learned to ride. She suffered a major head injury (which put her in a coma for some time), a hip fracture, and a broken femur. Thankfully she made a complete recovery and has no residual effects today. Their youngest son, who had Down syndrome, died in 1982 at the age of two from complications of a blood disorder that may have been unrelated to the condition. Another tragic event for Jim was his father's death when Jim was in the sixth grade. There were more, but you get the point.

Many families would have been devastated by such events. But Jim and Cille managed their lives with great poise, purpose, and strength. It was clear that Jim was relying on a great faith to undergird him. Never did I hear him complain or argue with reality. Not once did I observe him seeking sympathy from others, although he certainly didn't isolate himself from those closest to him. He and Cille were great examples of what it means to walk maturely in love—before, during, and after tragedy.

It wasn't too long after the fire that the Lord gave me the very same presence of mind that Jim Rewalt displayed. I'm not trying to suggest that the road has been easy by any means; at times it has been discouraging and downright difficult. What I'm suggesting is that no matter what, God has been with us every step of the way as a joyful companion. I've said many times that while I wouldn't wish this kind of tragedy on anyone else, I also wouldn't trade places with anyone. The growth in me has been nothing short of remarkable.

What's interesting is that our neighbor Susan (whose house was untouched by the fire) didn't fare so well. When we first knocked on her door to let her know we were alright, her face was pale as a ghost. She announced both her sorrow for our losses and that she had the worst case of survivor's guilt ever. We ended up consoling *her*, rather than the other way around.

Musing on the Word *So* -- a Rabbit Trail

What an interesting word—*so*—of which I became *so* consciously aware after the fire! It seems to be very useful as the start to just about any question. Many people who have no idea what to say will almost instinctively begin questions with that particular word:

"*So*, how are you guys doing?"

"*So*, did you recover much of value?"

"*So*, have you decided to rebuild?"

"*So*, where are you staying?"

"*So*, is your insurance company taking care of things for you?"

So—why did I bother to bring this up?

I can't really say, except I'm discovering that this word may very well be the most versatile in the entire English dictionary.

What I Need to Let Go of:

Fear of Being Alone

Back in 1980, just after my conversion to Christianity (and my divorce), I knew I wanted to marry Nancy, who hadn't been previously married. I'd like to say that God placed that knowledge and desire in me, but frankly I couldn't really know that at the time. Of course, now I *know* it was God; time has a way of cementing certain things. Nevertheless, I told her early on that I wanted to marry her.

In response, Nancy informed me that while she felt the same way, she absolutely would not marry me for at least a year. Why, I asked. She said I must live on my own for a year and *honestly* (a key word) be able to look her in the eye and announce that I could live the rest of my life *happily* unmarried if that's what God wanted for me.

You've got to be kidding, I thought. *Live alone for a year? Happily?* I wasn't sure I could do that. I was sure I didn't *want* to do that. You see, I was lonely after separating from Becky, and I didn't want to live by myself.

But I agreed to Nancy's request—I admired her that much.

It wasn't an easy year, but it was an extraordinarily valuable one. I learned that I *could* be joyful all by myself—as long as God was present. While I still struggle at times with not wanting to be alone, more and more I'm realizing that as long as God is with me (and I know, intellectually, that He always is), then that's enough. I don't need anything or anyone else.

Perhaps Nancy's request and my experience in that year had a lot to with our being married 38 years now.

Tragedy involving loss—whether of property or a relationship—has a way of making us feel alone. We wonder if we'll find security, love, or wholeness again. Some go deep into depression, causing concern for friends and family. I observed the same tendency in my own life following the fire. Would I ever live in my own home again? Have I disappointed God in such a way that He allowed this to happen? Am I getting what I deserve? Has He withdrawn the Holy Spirit from me?

Here are some powerful Scripture verses that counter such thinking. Each has served to encourage me at various times throughout this journey:

> I lift up my eyes to the hills—where does my help come from? My help comes from the LORD, the Maker of heaven and earth. (Psalm 121:1-2)

Do not let your hearts be troubled. Trust in God; trust also in me. (John 14:1)

Come to me, all you who are weary and burdened, and I will give you rest. Take my yoke upon you and learn from me, for I am gentle and humble in heart, and you will find rest for your souls. For my yoke is easy and my burden is light. (Matthew 11:28-30)

Cast all your anxiety on Him because He cares for you. (1 Peter 5:7)

God has said, "Never will I leave you; never will I forsake you." (Hebrews 13:5)

Be strong and courageous. Do not be afraid or terrified because of them, for the LORD your God goes with you; He will never leave you nor forsake you. (Deuteronomy 31:6)

It didn't take long for me to realize that God neither caused our tragedy nor was He punishing me through it. But He *was* using it mightily in my personal growth and for use in the kingdom. Tullian Tchividjian wrote a book entitled *Jesus + Nothing = Everything*. What an apt title! When we have Jesus, we *really* don't need anything or anyone else. We're *never* alone!

Application Questions about Tragedy

1. What has been the most dreadful tragedy you've experienced, or the most dreadful tragedy experienced by someone close to you? What were your immediate thoughts? Recount the timeline of events and, most importantly, how these things prompted you (or others) to move either toward God or away from Him.

2. Does God abandon His children in the midst of their tragedies? Does He really care? Why does He allow tragedy to occur in the lives of His children?

3. Has something in your life wounded you emotionally, physically, sexually, or spiritually? Have you experienced rejection, abandonment, neglect, or betrayal? Have you experienced a serious loss such as abortion, death of a loved one, adultery, divorce, job loss, or major illness? Is it possible to be truly and totally healed, restored, or reconciled to God after any of these?

4. Are you suffering with grief or pain (physical, mental, or emotional) at this time? What avoidance techniques have you developed when faced with grief or pain?

Do you believe God can heal the pain or remove the suffering? Have you been willing to simply push through the pain, believing that God would see you through? What was the result?

5. Are you afraid to be alone? What's the longest period you've ever been truly alone? What were your thoughts during this time? Were you able to draw comfort in some way? How?

6. Do you ever fear that the world is falling apart, that its values are becoming increasingly different from yours? Are you concerned that your country's leaders seem to be departing from the principles of our founding fathers? Do you fear that something really disastrous may occur nationally that could impact your personal security or way of life?

7. Do you know someone who seems to complain all the time? What's it like to be around this person? Are *you* prone to complaining? Do you find yourself overly sensitive in any particular area? Are you easily hurt emotionally? Why do you suppose that is, and what can you do about it?

What I Think

Do not conform any longer to the pattern of this world,
but be transformed by the renewing of your mind.
Then you will be able to test and approve what God's will is—
his good, pleasing, and perfect will.
ROMANS 12:2

We demolish arguments and every pretension that sets itself up
against the knowledge of God, and we take captive every thought
to make it obedient to Christ.
2 CORINTHIANS 10:5

Finally, brothers, whatever is true, whatever is noble,
whatever is right,
whatever is pure, whatever is lovely, whatever is admirable—
if anything is excellent or praiseworthy—think about such things.
PHILIPPIANS 4:6-8

My thinking is all screwed up! No kidding. *Stinkin' thinkin'*—you might say.

How do I know this and so confidently proclaim it? *Experience.*

As I look back on my major life decisions, I see that many of them were just plain bad. Not that bad decisions cannot be redeemed for my good, as Paul tells us:

> And we know that in all things God works for the good of those who love Him, who have been called according to His purpose. (Romans 8:28)

It's just that bad decisions are made from unqualified (baseless) thinking. Having a "gut feel" is little more than flipping a coin. My thinking, without the Lord's guidance and His Word, is like a boat without a rudder; it just drifts along with the prevailing current without any real direction. That's why God has given us the Bible as a manual for life. He tells us who we are, and He wants us to walk in that identity.

Read Ephesians 1, and it's plain to see that it's written largely in the past tense (emphasized by italicized words below); God is telling us what has *already* occurred. He's inviting us to believe it.

> Paul, an apostle of Christ Jesus by the will of God, To God's holy people in Ephesus, the faithful in Christ Jesus:
>
> Grace and peace to you from God our Father and the Lord Jesus Christ.
>
> Praise be to the God and Father of our Lord Jesus Christ, *who has blessed* us in the heavenly realms with every spiritual blessing in Christ. For *he chose* us in him before the creation of the world to be holy and blameless in his sight. In love

he predestined us for adoption to sonship through Jesus Christ, in accordance with his pleasure and will— to the praise of his glorious grace, which he *has freely given* us in the One he loves. In him *we have redemption* through his blood, the forgiveness of sins, in accordance with the riches of God's grace that *he lavished* on us. With all wisdom and understanding, *he made known* to us the mystery of his will according to his good pleasure, which *he purposed* in Christ, to be put into effect when the times reach their fulfillment—to bring unity to all things in heaven and on earth under Christ.

In him *we were also chosen, having been predestined* according to the plan of him who works out everything in conformity with the purpose of his will, in order that we, who were the first to put our hope in Christ, might be for the praise of his glory. And *you also were included* in Christ when you heard the message of truth, the gospel of your salvation. When you believed, *you were marked* in him with a seal, the promised Holy Spirit, who is a deposit guaranteeing our inheritance until the redemption of those who are God's possession—to the praise of his glory.…

And *God placed all things under his feet* and appointed him to be head over everything for the church, which is his body, the fullness of him who fills everything in every way.

Elsewhere, Paul says this:

Therefore, if anyone is in Christ, the *new creation has come*: *The old has gone*, the new is here! (2 Corinthians 5:17)

Why do we have such trouble believing God? In light of these great truths, why do we still insist on performing to earn His favor?

It seems we feel this way only to the degree that we haven't appropriated these truths into our thinking. I'm becoming convinced that our primary job as His children is to avidly devour His Word and allow it to mold our thinking, then walk obediently in what He says is true about us. It almost seems too simple. But the more quickly and efficiently we do that, the better off we are, and the more effective our Christian walk will be.

Succinctly stated, I'm learning this truth:

**I am not defined by what I think;
rather, I'm defined by what He thinks.**

It serves us well to learn His Word; Scripture itself admonishes us to do so:

> I have hidden your word in my heart that I might not sin against you. (Psalm 119:11)

> All Scripture is God-breathed and is useful for teaching, rebuking, correcting, and training in righteousness, so that the man of God may be thoroughly equipped for every good work. (2 Timothy 3:16-17)

These are just two verses, one each from the Old and New Testaments, but there are many other references that emphasize the importance of learning the Scriptures. Luke commended the Berean church for doing just that:

Now the Bereans were of more noble character than the Thessalonians, for they received the message with great eagerness and examined the Scriptures every day to see if what Paul said was true. (Acts 17:11)

Just for kicks, I once examined Psalm 119 (which emphasizes the importance of our meditating on and learning God's Word) and counted the number of times a term was used that signifies either the law of God or His Word. The results were surprising:

term:	occurrences:
law	45
word	28
statute	23
command, commandment	22
decree	22
precept	21

That's 161 occurrences in all! Profound, wouldn't you agree? It turned out *not* to be a meaningless exercise after all.

Think about it for a moment: when we buy a new appliance, the first thing we should review is the instruction manual so we know how to operate it properly. That just makes sense. After buying a new car, it's vital to read the owner's manual to become acquainted with all its features. And when we purchase a new computer or peripheral, it's important to familiarize ourselves with all its capabilities.

The Bible has been likened to a manual for *life* itself. The better we acquaint ourselves with this manual, the smoother our lives will run.

I find in my life experience that when I rely on my own wisdom in making decisions, things don't always turn out as I'd planned. And when I rely on God's Word in making decisions, things always turn out as planned, right? Wrong! But at least I know that God is using everything to accomplish His purposes. And here, it's worth repeating Romans 8:28:

> And we know that in all things God works for the good of those who love Him, who have been called according to His purpose.

It's just plain better when we include God in our plans. And better yet when we invite Him to make our plans for us.

When we don't include God in our plans, I've learned we're asking for trouble, largely because we move away from His protective cover. This represents a subtle (or not so subtle) form of rebellion when we don't include Him. It's like a Little League baseball team ignoring the coach's instructions (if you've ever seen it, you know exactly what I'm talking about!). The result can be utter chaos.

Our sincerity has nothing to do with it. Sometimes people mistake sincerity for hearing from God. I've known those who've studied a situation at length and made decisions in all sincerity, but they were sincerely wrong. They neglected to include God in the decision-making process. It's always better to have the head attached to the body.

When I worked at Air Force Space Command, I had the opportunity on numerous occasions to brief the director of operations, Brigadier General Ronald Gray. General Gray had the reputation of being a real hard-nosed leader, and most junior officers feared briefing him. I'd seen him chew an underling up and down in the course of a couple of minutes. He was a bright man, but skeptical and discerning as he received a briefing. His language was often colorful. He would tell a young officer who wasn't clear on his facts, "You, know, lieutenant, I may have been born at night, but I wasn't born *last* night!"

General Gray is now an optometry patient of mine as well as my friend. I remember once reminding him how most of my colleagues feared briefing him, but I never really did. I wondered if he knew why.

His answer was interesting. "Because you, John, knew what the hell you were talking about!"

As I've thought about his comment, the only thing that comes to mind is that I always sought the Lord's wisdom in prayer before I went in to brief him. Might the Lord have calmed me, given me a sense of confidence, shared His wisdom, and briefed the general through me? Very likely. What else could it be? I certainly didn't view myself as being smarter than any of the other officers who briefed him.

What I Need to Let Go of:

Entertaining (Dwelling on) Below-the-Line Thinking

Scripture encourages us to think healthy, positive thoughts—as we see in the flagship verses highlighted at the beginning of this chapter. So why is it so easy to dwell on the opposite type of thoughts—the unhealthy and negative ones?

I don't know. But I do know I'm very good at doing just that.

A lot has been written about negative thinking patterns. The following common categories have been identified (adapted from a list compiled by Wesley Wilson, LMFT):

1. *Catastrophizing*—taking a relatively minor event and imagining all sorts of terrors and awful scenarios that could result from it (making a mountain out of a molehill). Nancy has a great expression for this; she calls it *awfulizing*.

2. *All-or-nothing thinking*—"black or white" thinking which focuses on the extremes. It assumes that situations are either entirely good or entirely bad, with no in-between or gray areas.

3. *Making demands*—expecting, even demanding (from yourself as well as others) that your rules be followed and never broken. These are demands, not preferences.

4. *Fortune-telling*—prophesying what the outcome will be before it happens. This can prevent any risk-taking.

5. *Mind-reading*—negative judgmental assumptions of what others are thinking. This can result in social anxiety and relationship ruptures.

6. *Emotional reasoning*—blindly believing that our strong feelings must be a true reflection of what's going on in reality.

7. *Over-generalizing*—making widespread judgments about yourself, others, or the world on the strength of one or two particular features.

8. *Labeling*—calling yourself, others, and the world cruel or nasty names.

9. *Mental filtering*—letting through only the information that fits with what you already believe about yourself, others, or the world. This leads to biased and negative viewpoints.

10. *Disqualifying the positive* (similar to mental filtering)— distorting new or positive information into something you believe is negative or harmful.

11. *Low-frustration tolerance*—equating "uncomfortable" with "unbearable." You're likely to give up striving toward your goals whenever the going gets too tough or painful.

12. *Personalizing*—taking random events and making them a personal issue. Everything that happens around you becomes about *you*, regardless of how strongly reality indicates otherwise.

Over the years, I've fallen into each of these negative ways of thinking, with particularly strong fluency in numbers 1, 2, 5, and 7. All of these mental approaches can lead to ineffectiveness, ill will, bitterness, resentment, and paralysis—not fun by any stretch.

Nelson Mandela once said that "resentment is like drinking poison and then hoping it will kill your enemies." How often do we think just like that?

What I'm learning is that I can, in fact, exercise some control over my thinking and choose not only what *not* to think, but instead what *to* think.

Shifting My Thinking

Nancy and I attended a four-day workshop in Denver hosted by Gary and Cathy Hawk of Clarity, International. It was eye-opening, to say the least. During the workshop we learned much about our own thinking patterns, particularly where our negative thinking was most likely to take us. For me, the dangers are anxiety, resentment, evaluating, withdrawal, passivity, control, and pressure.

We then learned how to recognize when we were entertaining such below-the-line (BTL) thoughts, and were given tools to show us how to shift to above-the-line (ATL) thinking. As an example, when I'm stuck in anxiety, I've learned to shift to thoughts of enthusiasm. This sort of conscious awareness really works, and helps me move quickly from BTL to ATL thinking.

I still find myself tending toward negative thoughts at times, but by and large I'm doing much better than before. It takes some work—a concerted effort to think more on the positive and less on the negative.

The Clarity approach is a worldly attempt to exercise a godly principle. Consider the following Scripture verses (some of my personal favorites):

> As a man thinketh in his heart, so is he. (Proverbs 23:7, KJV)

> We demolish arguments and every pretension that sets itself up against the knowledge of God, and we take captive every thought to make it obedient to Christ. (2 Corinthians 10:4-5)

> Finally, brothers and sisters, whatever is true, whatever is noble, whatever is right, whatever is pure, whatever is lovely, whatever is admirable— if anything is excellent or praiseworthy—think about such things. (Philippians 4:8)

James Allen sums it up quite nicely in *As a Man Thinketh* (written more than a century ago): "As he thinks, so he is; as he continues to think, so he remains."

The Lord once gave me the following:

> The Christian life is *not* one of me *becoming* a better person—it's one of *discovering* the person God *already sees me as.*

More and more I'm learning that the Christian life is one of *discovery*. God desires all His children to discover who He has made them to be in Christ, and then to *walk in who they already are.*

Thomas Merton captured it beautifully: "Finally I am coming to the conclusion that my highest ambition is to be what I already am."

There's nothing we can do to make ourselves more lovable, more righteous, or more deserving in God's eyes (as much as this flies in the face of conventional thinking)—so we might just as well accept it and move on as though it were really true—because it is!

Application Questions about What I Think

1. Name one of your core beliefs that you had carried for a long time before it changed dramatically. What occurred to bring about this change? What belief are you holding onto now that could, and should, be changed in the future?

2. Have you ever asked yourself, "Why would I go along with that kind of wrong thinking?"

3. Have you ever thought about what kinds of truth you're living by? Are you honest with yourself about what you think and believe? Do you have a peaceful mind that knows the truth?

4. Of the twelve categories of below-the-line thinking mentioned in this chapter, which do you fall into most easily? What techniques have you developed for pulling yourself out of such thinking? Do they work? What might be more effective?

5. Can the Scriptures be trusted? Are they entirely believable? Do they represent absolute truth? Are they relevant to your daily living?

6. What do you do when a Scripture doesn't make sense to you? What *should* you do? Is there a logical explanation for every difficult verse, or is it okay to ignore some of them as perhaps being mistaken?

7. Write down what you believe to be absolutely true about God (the more exhaustive the list, the better). How can this list impact your daily living? Why is it so hard to keep this list at the forefront of our minds while we go about our daily living?

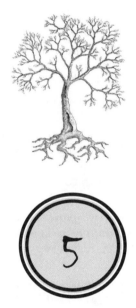

What Others Think

Am I now trying to win the approval of men, or of God?
Or am I trying to please men? If I were still trying to please men,
I would not be a servant of Christ.
GALATIANS 1:10

On the contrary, we speak as men approved by God to be
entrusted with the gospel.
We are not trying to please men but God, who tests our hearts.
1 THESSALONIANS 2:4

Fear of man will prove to be a snare,
but whoever trusts in the LORD is kept safe.
PROVERBS 29:25

Peter and the other apostles replied:
"We must obey God rather than men!"
ACTS 5:29

When I was little, some friends persuaded my cousin Steve and me to join them on a hike into some foothills near my home. It was a tiring hike, but the view from the top was exhilarating. We were on top of the world! After admiring our kingdom for awhile, one of the boys produced a pack of cigarettes he'd stolen from his dad's stash. They were unlike any I'd ever seen; they were black in color.

I'd never smoked before, and certainly had no intention of smoking then. But young mischievous boys have a way of persuading you to do something that may not be good for you. When they pulled out a box of matches and suggested I try one, I felt nervous but nevertheless went along with the rest of the crowd. I smoked one. Then another. Then one more, mostly to "fit in."

Later that afternoon I became sick to my stomach, which turned out to be a good thing in that I've never desired to smoke again. But I began to realize even then how vulnerable I am to what others think.

Many of my early views in life came from my friends and family, and in a way that's what one would expect. However, not all those assimilated views reflect truth, and they can lead us into unwholesome decisions.

After becoming a Christian I became aware of a guide that contains ultimate truth and can thus be wholly trusted: the Bible, God's manual for our daily living. It's refashioning my thinking and has never let me down.

It's convincing me of this truth:

> **I am not defined by what others think;**
> **rather, I'm defined by what He thinks.**

It hasn't happened all at once, and I haven't arrived, to be sure. At times I still struggle with what others think, but it's certainly improving.

The following story demonstrates this point.

An Optometry School Challenge

This particular challenge occurred during one of my optometry rotations, or externships, as we called them. Most optometry students do a total of four three-month rotations during their final year to get clinical experience. I had two pediatric rotations scheduled and felt I could use more experience in disease management, so I convinced a classmate to trade me his VA (Veterans Administration) rotation for one of my pediatric rotations. My undergraduate background was mostly hard sciences, with special emphasis in math and physics. My background in the health sciences was, consequently, poor. That didn't stop me, however, from believing I could successfully accomplish such a difficult rotation.

To obtain approval for this swap, I visited the preceptor for the Bedford VA optometry clinic. His name was Dr. Rodney Gutner and he had a reputation as being an exceptional VA health provider. He also had a reputation of intensely disliking the accelerated program I was in, and he had no reservations about sharing that sentiment. He said it would be fine for me to work under his guidance, but his goal was to *fail* me.

Perhaps that should have given me pause. But in my overconfidence, I took it as a challenge. I told Dr. Gutner that I was not only up to the task, but looking forward to it.

My, what a difficult rotation it turned out to be! It would have been extraordinarily difficult even without Dr. Gutner's "help." He not only reminded me periodically that his goal was to fail me, but he seemed to work hard to facilitate that outcome along the way.

He would often enter the exam room about the time I was finalizing a patient's prescription, then signal me to step aside while he verified it. His result was always quite different than mine, and then he would throw me a puzzled look with his hands facing up, as if to say, "What's wrong with you?"

He encouraged a young assistant, a relatively new optometrist, to do the same thing at times. It was extremely unsettling, and gradually served to erode my self-confidence. My sleep became progressively worse. I lay in bed at night wondering what was wrong with me. I even went to see a psychiatrist who wanted to put me on medication, which I refused to allow.

The last day of the rotation—the big day for final grades—arrived, bringing trepidation on my part after another night of little sleep. Dr. Gutner and his assistant met with me and told me that not only had I failed the rotation, but I should probably consider a different career path – optometry *wasn't for me*.

Somehow, I wasn't terribly surprised with the news. What surprised me was my response: I said that I appreciated very much both the experience and Dr. Gutner himself, and I had absolutely no intention of giving up on optometry. Instead, I would persevere to become as good an optometrist as he was.

That had to come from God!

Dr. Gutner's mouth dropped just before he announced, "Don't you understand? I just failed you!"

"I understand," I responded, "but I intend to use this experience to help me become a great O.D.!"

The stigma of failing a rotation wasn't nearly as bad as I thought it might be; after all, I wasn't the first to fail a Bedford VA rotation (nor the last, I suppose). It turned out to be a blessing in disguise, as I discovered during a make-up rotation. I was placed under the tutelage of Dr. Walter Potazniak at one of the community health centers. He had a reputation of being very good with people (like me) who had confidence problems.

And did he ever come through for me! He sat me down before the rotation began and said he believed in me. He gave me a book to read on being a good clinician, and said he'd be working very closely with me to ensure my success. His attitude made a huge difference for me. I was working alongside five other students, and by the end of the rotation, several asked me how I was doing so well. They asked if they could watch as I performed exams so they could become better clinicians. That alone was a confidence-booster that made me feel very good.

Of course I had to successfully complete an additional rotation to make up for the one I failed. I had no say whatever about what or where it would be, and I was told it would be at the VA Hospital in Providence, Rhode Island. I learned that the preceptor there was a retired Army colonel with a similar reputation to Dr. Gutner's. *Oh, great,* I thought. But when I talked with this colonel prior to the rotation (he knew about my rotation at the Bedford VA), he assured me that he'd treat me fairly, although I'd have to *perform*. He'd view my situation no differently than any other student. That's all I could possibly want.

I did well during the rotation, and I believed this preceptor was pleased with my performance. My family had moved back to Colorado Springs during this time, and I missed them a great deal—so much so that I asked the preceptor if there was any way I might finish the rotation a bit early to join my family for Thanksgiving. He noted that it was an unusual request, and that he'd have to give it some thought.

The next day he stormed into the exam room where I was at the biomicroscope evaluating a patient's eyes.

He said loudly, "RABINS!"

"Yes, sir," I replied.

"YOU PASSED!" Probably the most beautiful words I've ever heard, words that launched me confidently into an incredible career as an optometrist.

What I Need to Let Go of:

Feelings of Rejection

As I look back on many of my life decisions, even those as a Christian, I see an embarrassing pattern of attempting to avoid rejection. It's as though being rejected is the worst thing that could happen to me; thus many of the decisions I've made have served to steer clear of that feeling. Even my addictive behaviors have served to "alleviate" feelings of rejection, at least for a time. But those who struggle with addiction know that on emerging from the behavior, we're confronted with the same problems, fears, feelings, and anxieties that we were attempting to avoid through the behavior. They haven't gone anywhere; *we* have!

A positive and motivational quote in big letters at the Cheyenne Mountain Re-entry Center (a local medium-security prison) expressed it well:

THERE IS NOTHING SO BAD THAT A RELAPSE WON'T MAKE IT WORSE!

Here's an important fact—God does *not* reject us! He promises in His Word:

> For the LORD will not reject his people; he will never forsake his inheritance. (Psalm 94:14)

I'm learning not to fear rejection from others or to view it as an indictment on me personally. Rather, I'm learning to face my emotions and pain in a more mature, healthy manner than I have in the past. Consequently, my decisions are becoming more in line with what God thinks of me, and I'm growing as a result.

God truly is the only One who can say, "I love you *just* the way you are, but I love you too much to leave you there."

I love where I am and what God is doing in my life *right now.*

Application Questions about What Others Think

1. Recount a time when you went along with group or peer pressure, knowing deep down that it was wrong. Later on, how did you feel about it, and about yourself? How did you respond? Why do we find it difficult to speak up for truth in the face of opposition?

2. Recall a time when you applied undue pressure on someone else to do something they felt was wrong. What were the consequences? Did that person ever confront you about what you did? Should you have been confronted? Does anything come to mind now about what you might do to make amends?

3. Who in your life has influenced you the most, especially in forming the life views you now hold? How do you feel about that person today? Do you respect or resent him or her? Why?

4. Do you feel as though you sometimes relate to others from a posture of fear instead of grace, mercy, honesty,

truth, joy, and love? How might you move away from fear toward something better?

5. Who in your life knows you best—your strengths as well as your weaknesses? What is it about that person that allows you to be vulnerable? What is it about yourself that keeps you from being more vulnerable with others?

6. Think once again about someone who knows you best—the person you're most vulnerable with. In spite of this vulnerability, what are you hiding from this person? What do you want to share with this person that you're afraid to, simply because you fear rejection? What secrets are you keeping to yourself? Is it possible you're keeping some secrets from yourself, perpetuating a state of denial?

7. What is God doing in your life right now that convinces you not only that He loves you, but that what He thinks about you is supremely important?

What I Control

Rejoice in the Lord always. I will say it again: Rejoice!
Let your gentleness be evident to all. The Lord is near.
Do not be anxious about anything, but in everything,
by prayer and petition, with thanksgiving, present your requests to God.
And the peace of God, which transcends all understanding,
will guard your hearts and your minds in Christ Jesus.
PHILIPPIANS 4:4-7

Who of you by worrying can add a single hour to his life?
MATTHEW 6:27

Trust in the LORD *with all your heart and lean*
not on your own understanding:
in all your ways acknowledge him, and he will make your paths straight.
PROVERBS 3:5-6

Sometimes the Lord calms the storm. More often,
He lets the storm rage and calms His child.
Now relax in the Lord!
FELLOW CHURCH MEMBER IN ALBUQUERQUE

I've always had great control of my life circumstances. Or so I thought—until I became painfully aware of some addictive behavior and thinking that threw me totally out of control.

Let's preface this chapter by recognizing that the word "control" is an interesting one to say the least. Depending on the situation, someone "in control" may truly be enslaved to a harmful behavior pattern, while another person "out of control" may be totally relying upon God for direction. Consequently, "control" may be healthy or unhealthy, and the word itself is ambiguous at best.

I think what it boils down to is this: Who, exactly, is doing the controlling?

If *I* am, then I must conclude that God isn't—and that's not a healthy form of control. But if I allow God to control my life, that leaves me out of control, and that seems to be quite healthy.

Of course one could argue that even when I'm in control, I'm really *not*; I only think I am.

Oh, this can be so confusing! I never seem to get anywhere with it, so let's move on.

Addiction and Control

Addictive behaviors and thought patterns are often accompanied by unrealistic, fantasy-laden dreams in which one controls the future and attaches to the outcome. One might logically think I'm an expert in the area of addiction in that I've struggled with it for much of my life. But just because I'm good at something doesn't make me an expert. If I were truly an expert, I'd have probably figured out years ago how to avoid, or at least control, the addictive behavior.

Having said that, let me add that I've no intention of talking about my own personal brand of addiction; perhaps that's the subject of another book. This section is for all who struggle with addiction of any kind, whether it be alcohol, cigarettes, sex, food, narcotics, or a whole host of other possibilities. I honestly think that everyone has some form(s) of addictive behavior; many just don't realize it. Those who do realize it and work to overcome it may easily fall prey to another addiction; it's easy to trade one addiction for another.

All addiction affects the same part of the brain, principally the limbic system. So it totally escapes me why one person struggles with alcohol and yet has no attraction to cigarettes, while another struggles with pornography but has no interest in alcohol.

Here's another thought I struggle with concerning addiction and Christian faith. It has to do with faith in God who loves me unconditionally, who died for me, who petitions on my behalf, and who *lives within me*. That last part is what gets me—the part about Jesus living in me. If I *really* believed that, I wonder why I continue to behave the way I do. It seems to me as though I become practically an unbeliever when I walk in addiction. It certainly makes me seem hypocritical at best.

A friend recently confided that he'd relapsed after a full year of sobriety. But he shared that he experienced a great deal of serenity after repenting and re-surrendering to the Lord. He asked me for advice and to pray for him. In my quiet time alone with the Lord the next day, He reminded me of something very important, which I promptly shared with my friend. Here's what the Lord had me write down:

> The serenity you shared intrigued me. You see, many have claimed we shouldn't act out because of the way we feel AFTER. It's true that we feel badly after relapsing. However, I think they have it backwards. More appropriate, I think, is the following:

Rather than our feelings toward God depending on our acting out, I think more importantly our acting out reflects our feelings toward God (specifically our relationship with Him). Something to think about.

My friend wrote back, "After this weekend I concur with your point unreservedly."

Working under contract with the Colorado Department of Corrections to regularly perform eye exams for prison inmates has raised another interesting dilemma that pops up about addiction. It has to do with freedom. I'm convinced that in spite of the physical bars, some prisoners are *more free* inside their prison bars than I am "out there" when I'm walking in addiction. The only difference is that I "carry my bars" with me. This concept intrigues and challenges me.

I'm reminded of a passage from the New Testament in which Paul laments what I personally think amounts to an addiction:

> Therefore, in order to keep me from becoming conceited, I was given a thorn in my flesh, a messenger of Satan, to torment me. Three times I pleaded with the Lord to take it away from me. But he said to me, "My grace is sufficient for you, for my power is made perfect in weakness." Therefore I will boast all the more gladly about my weaknesses, so that Christ's power may rest on me. That is why, for Christ's sake, I delight in weaknesses, in insults, in hardships, in persecutions, in difficulties. For when I am weak, then I am strong. (2 Corinthians 12:7-10)

I admit that my assessment of Paul's affliction may be wrong. A number of theories have been posited, poor eyesight being just one of them. I don't think the Scripture's failure to identify what Paul struggled with is important. Here's why: I see Paul as struggling with exactly the same thing as I do. I think God intentionally wrote this passage through Paul in such a way that each addict will see Paul as addicted to the same thing he or she is. Isn't that just like a loving God—to allow us to see ourselves through a great man of God who's struggling with the same things we struggle with?

Jesus himself endured temptations common to man, yet never succumbed to sin. No matter our weakness, we overcome by trusting God to be our strength. I've taken liberty to modify the last part of the 1 Corinthians passage above by putting it thus:

> In *my* strength, I'm weak, but in my weakness, He
> is strong, when I allow Him to be.

The important take-away for me from this section is that addiction has taught me that I'm out of control in at least one area of my life. As long as I'm in control in most other areas, however, I should be okay, right? Wrong!

Here are three important lessons worthy of consideration when it comes to control:

1. While goals are good, I'm to enjoy the journey more and the destination less, leaving that in God's hands.

2. I shouldn't compartmentalize my life to the point of convincing myself that God is separate (or even absent) from any aspect of my life.

3. I must choose to face life's problems maturely, and not throw up my hands and say, "Oh, well, I have an

addiction," but instead make godly, obedient choices in spite of past failures.

Total Control (Fantasy), Partial Control (Awakening), No Control (Reality)

Losing our home and the rental property, along with most of our personal belongings, made me reflect upon how little I really do control. The fact is that I probably control nothing, except perhaps my will and thoughts. While I have to remind myself frequently of this, what's comforting is that I can release any anxiety associated with feeling out of control by pondering this truth:

I am not defined by what I control (or *think* I control); rather, I'm defined by Him who controls everything.

Back to control again. When we feed an addiction, it's as though we attempt to control a small area of behavior that we keep just to ourselves. It's how Gollum in *The Lord of the Rings* must have felt about "my precious," a golden ring he never really owned. The sad part is that while we think we're in control of this one area, we're really out of control—and *it* controls us! Until we realize how out of control we are, we cannot surrender that area to the only One who's truly able to control it.

I see in myself the desire to control not only personal behaviors but also behaviors in others. How ludicrous to think I might control in someone else something that I can't control even in me! To my chagrin, I see that tendency in me. Even worse, I see myself attempting to create for myself and others a future outcome often steeped in fantasy. There's simply no real satisfaction in that, and (again) I'm learning that I must enjoy the outcome less and the journey more.

God has each one of us on a path, and He promises to walk that path beside us. How comforting it is when we trust Him to do that. I don't have to attach to a particular outcome, but rather walk in obedience, enjoying the journey and basking in His presence as I travel. When I'm able to truly grasp the importance of this, dreams of future fantasy, controlling another's destiny, and anxiety over what might happen all tend to vanish.

Byron Katie—at the beginning of chapter 11 in *Who Would You Be Without Your Story?*—sums this up nicely: "Once you realize that you've been living with a fantasy, you may discover someone you can love with all your heart. That someone is *you*. This is the key to all relationships."

I would add that this "someone" is precisely who God made you to be.

What I Need to Let Go of:

Addictive Behaviors and Thought Patterns with Accompanying Unrealistic, Fantasy-Laden Dreams Whereby I Control the Future and Attach to the outcome

Here comes some frank self-disclosure. As I thought and prayed about my personal brand of addiction some time ago, the Lord brought to mind many other habitual behaviors that are a big part of my daily living—things that I do everyday. These behaviors include reading the newspaper, working the daily crossword puzzle, exercising, checking my weight, checking my investment portfolios, checking my emails, listening to the radio while driving, and having my cell phone always available for calls and texts. Even Bible study and devotions had become ritualistic and habitual for me. I have actually experienced anxiety if I didn't accomplish one of these activities. They'd become things I felt I needed to get through in order to get on with the day. There are undoubtedly more, but these are what came to mind on first blush.

Of course none of these activities would be necessarily considered "sinful" in and of themselves. In moderation, none of them seems to be a problem for most people. Some of them are actually considered to be good habits, like Bible study and physical exercise. But studying the Bible without connecting with the Holy God who wrote it is surely missing its primary value. And it's a bit embarrassing when I think of how often I would ritualistically engage in some of the other activities. For instance, at times I'd weigh myself multiple times during the day—at home first thing in the morning, then at the gym, and occasionally at the office. And once wasn't generally enough at any of these venues. Same with checking on my portfolios, emails, and texts.

It occurred to me that these activities must have provided me some sense of comfort, stability, or security. But true joy doesn't come from any of these activities, so I asked the Lord to help me with an experiment designed to help me discover true joy and intimacy with Him.

I decided to give up all of these activities and food (but not my devotions) for thirty-six hours. No eating; no newspaper or crossword puzzle; no checking my weight, portfolios, emails, or texts; and no radio in the car. I seriously questioned whether I could, in fact, do this, so I surrendered the plan to God, asking Him to help me and teach me through it.

A friend asked me why I couldn't check my weight or stocks just once a day. Why couldn't I just do things in moderation? I responded that I obviously wasn't normal and had to make a complete break from these things in order to succeed with the experiment. So beginning after dinner on a Monday evening I embarked on the plan.

Tuesday morning was interesting, to say the least. After waking and using the bathroom, I headed straight to the scale, only then remembering that I wasn't weighing myself that day. I did my devotionals, then went into the kitchen for breakfast; oops, no breakfast, either. I remembered not to turn my cell phone on, so I didn't check emails or texts. To make sure I didn't slip, I put a small note on my cell phone: "You don't need this today." I put a similar note on the scales.

Nothing to do, I thought as I stood by my desk. *I cannot retrieve the paper, and I won't exercise.* So I got on my knees by the couch and prayed. I asked God to help me through the day and allow me to draw closer to Him. I remained in that position for some time, waiting for Him to speak to me. And He did! He told me how much He loved me and wanted to spend time with me. He encouraged me to do the experiment I'd set out to do, and He let me know that He'd be along to help me. He told me He was all I really needed, anyway, and would *prove* that to me as the day progressed.

At work I placed a note on my computer reminding me that I didn't need to check my emails. Only once did I forget, and I started to check, but very quickly closed out of the application. Talk about habituation! I left my cell phone on my desk to avoid any distraction as I was seeing patients or interacting with my staff. I remembered that I might be receiving an important email from an attorney, but reminded myself that nothing was so important that it couldn't wait a day.

And what a day it turned out to be! And what lessons I'm still gleaning from the experiment!

First of all, I didn't really miss the routine, habitual activities that had so defined my life to date. I didn't miss eating (I did drink water through the day). I was more focused and present with my patients and staff—they even told me this. I was much more productive between patient encounters, reviewing a large stack of professional journals that had been sitting for a month. Most importantly, I was more consciously aware of the presence of God throughout the day, frequently connecting with Him in prayer. I felt an intimacy with Him that was simply wonderful.

Later, at home, I was excited to share the day with Nancy and was certainly more present with her. I experienced firsthand this truth:

No Distractions = Better Relationships
with Others and with God

I slept very well the last night of the experiment and awoke the next morning wondering what God had in store for me. I weighed myself, then put a note on the scale indicating that once a day is enough. I'd lost three pounds, which was exciting for me. I ate a small breakfast but truly wasn't very hungry. My devotionals were more intentionally focused on communicating with God and enjoying intimacy with Him. I was so joyful! On checking my email after not doing so for thirty-six hours, I discovered *absolutely nothing* that was time-urgent. Within less than fifteen minutes I was caught up! I chose to not listen to the radio during the drive into the office, and I left my cell phone on my desk during patient encounters. I didn't weigh myself during the day.

I've decided to make some of these changes permanent. Truly I don't need to weigh myself more than once during the day; arguably I don't need to weigh more than once a week. But for now, once a day is just fine. And I've decided to leave my cell phone on my desk when I'm seeing patients. My emails and texts don't need the amount of attention they were getting before. I'm sure I'll recognize other changes over time that can be made.

At this point, I'd call the experiment an overwhelming success, and I plan to do it again from time to time. I'm excited to be on this current journey, enjoying a more intimate relationship with the One who loves me most—and who *really* is in control!

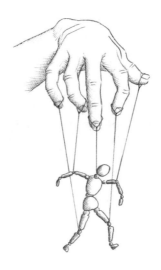

Application Questions about Control

1. What about your life do you feel you have the most control over? What would you *like* to have the most control over?

2. Do you do things you know are wrong, only to find yourself asking, "Why do I continue doing what I don't want to be doing?" How do you answer this question?

3. Do you struggle with addictive behaviors? Have you honestly looked at why you haven't succeeded at overcoming them? What would it take to do so?

4. Do you believe you have obstacles and barriers that are keeping you from succeeding in any area of your life? Are you willing to look at your life honestly? Are you ready to clear the path of what keeps you in bondage, and walk in freedom?

5. How do you cope with grief, disappointment, uncomfortable emotions, anxiety, anger, etc.? Is there a better way? How might you move toward that better way?

6. Does it comfort you to know that Paul struggled with a "thorn" (2 Corinthians 12:7)? What do *you* think this thorn actually was? How can you relate his struggle to your own life?

7. What would giving complete control of your life to God look like?

Who I Know

*For I resolved to know nothing while I was with you
except Jesus Christ and him crucified.*
1 CORINTHIANS 2:2

*Many seek an audience with a ruler,
but it is from the LORD that man gets justice.*
PROVERBS 29:26

I've always loved hanging around important people. When my sister Karen and I were little, our family had season tickets to all the musicals at the Ahmanson Theater in Los Angeles, and we saw musicals at other venues as well. We always waited for the stars of the show to exit the back of the theater so we could obtain their autographs on our printed programs. It made us feel particularly good when they actually addressed us by name atop their signatures. I got to meet Jay Leno once at a gas station in Simi Valley. He was driving one of the Stutz Bearcats from his famous automobile collection. Even though I'd only seen him on TV a couple of times, and frankly didn't care that much for him, I managed to tell him how much I appreciated his show.

In the Air Force, I had opportunities to brief dignitaries, ambassadors, politicians, and general officers. It always felt good to be acknowledged by someone of that stature, and it somehow made me feel important.

The problem with drawing my value from that class of people is that when they're not around or when they reject me, my self-esteem flags. Even well-intentioned people will eventually let you down -- it's simply part of being human. Only One loves us unconditionally, without respect to what we look like, what we've done, or who we know. His name is Jesus, and He values us based exclusively on what *He* has done and who *He* is.

Imagine that—someone who values me, adores me, blesses me, nurtures me, encourages me, strengthens me, abides in me, promises never to leave me…in spite of me!

Over time, I'm learning to appreciate the following truth:

**I am not defined by who I know;
rather, I'm defined by Him who knows me best.**

I'm also learning to appreciate how the relationships that matter most are those established by God, regardless of how "important" those people are in the eyes of the world. It turns out that some of the most important people I've met are simply not important at all in the world's view.

A few examples will illustrate this.

The Street Evangelist

When I was in my Ph.D. program, several of us would walk to a far corner of the campus during breaks to be "amused" by a street evangelist who showed up every day. He was of the loud, fire-and-brimstone variety, and he managed to irritate many an inquisitive onlooker. Some heckled him and some threw things at him, but that never deterred him from what he was doing.

What's interesting is that he was completely blind. When anyone threw something at him, he had no idea where it came from. But that didn't matter—he just kept going.

One day I felt nudged by the Lord to go up to him and encourage him. Naturally I thought I must be hearing things; God certainly wouldn't embarrass me by asking me to encourage someone whose methods I disagreed with. Besides, I was a fairly new believer, and my friends would think I was crazy. But God persisted, and I was naïve enough to believe Him.

I went up to the gentleman, standing before him a moment. He sensed someone there, stopped speaking to the crowd, and said, "What can I do for you?"

"Sir," I replied, "you don't know me, but I believe God wants me to tell you that He's pleased with you and wants me to encourage you."

Immediately tears flowed from his eyes and he wrapped his arms around me tightly, thanking me profusely. At that moment it didn't matter what my friends thought. All that mattered was that I'd stepped out in faith and was exactly where God wanted me to be in that moment.

> For we live by faith, not by sight. (2 Corinthians 5:7)

That experience taught me that God uses His children in various ways to further the gospel, not all of which are easy or to our liking.

The Hawaiian Photographer

A few months after the Black Forest fire, Nancy and I went to Hawaii to process and pray. We also dreamed and planned. We stayed at Bellows Air Force Station, a recreational base on the windward side of Oahu. Bellows has cabins on the beach that are wonderfully private. One day we went to one of the largest swap meets in the country, at Aloha Stadium. There were well over seven hundred vendors in booths surrounding the entire stadium. I was in no mood to buy anything, which was interesting in that I owned very little at this point. But I wanted nothing, really.

In one booth, I saw a small poster of Hanauma Bay at sunrise and asked the lady in the booth how much she wanted for it. "Fifteen dollars," she replied. Since haggling is encouraged at this swap meet, I told her I'd pay ten dollars for it. She yelled at me, calling me some names that I won't repeat here. That interaction surely didn't encourage me to buy anything.

Later we found an intriguing booth owned by a remarkable photographer named Brian Kusko. His photos were of natural scenery in the islands, principally waterfalls, waves, and bays. Lots of water. What distinguished his photos from many others was the metal substrate they were printed on, a process that serves to augment colors quite beautifully. Brian asked me what I was looking for, and I responded by asking if he had a sunrise shot of Hanauma Bay, our favorite spot to snorkel. He said that unfortunately he did not, but asked for my email address. I walked out of his booth saddened, because I'd still not found anything I wanted to buy.

The next day I received the following message from Brian, starting an email exchange reproduced here:

On Sep 2, 2013, at 9:08 AM, Brian wrote:

Hi, John,

It was a pleasure to meet you yesterday at the swap meet. I hope you are still enjoying your stay here on the islands! I'm dedicating this photo to you as it was you who inspired me to seek out this image. I feel that every great image has a great story:

It starts at the swap meet when we had our conversation. Right from that moment I decided I was going to go straight to Hanauma Bay after the swap meet and do some scouting. I did just that. I used to live in Hawaii Kai around the corner from Hanauma, so I know of a trail that is used by the county for maintenance. I have a handy little application on my phone that helps me pinpoint where the sun will be rising on any given day. Tools and knowledge in hand and mind, I trekked around the old crater rim in search of the best vantage point, snapping here, snapping there. I wandered from the trail a bit looking for the best possible angle, lost my footing, and went sliding down into the crater. I thudded to a stop in front of what seemed to be the only patch of flowers in the crater. I brushed myself off and took this shot... [not shown here is Brian's crude photo of the Bay]

I got up at 4:30 this morning and left Kailua to find that flower patch. It was pretty dark still and my little headlamp died right on the spot. Lucky for me and my 20/20 vision (I'm still going to have my eyes checked per your advice), I found them, being more careful this time on my approach so as not to ruin them in all their morning glory. I nestled up in the rocks, got my tripod set, and waited for the magic that the sun would bring. My dad was with me and he got a blurry shot with his point and shoot. .

And finally here is the image that you inspired, John. I'm simply calling it "Hanauma Sunrise"

It's going to look incredible on metal. Thank you!!!

On Sep 2, 2013, at 1:57 PM, I wrote:

I love it! I'd like to buy your very first-numbered unit on metal. What I don't think you know is that we recently lost our beautiful home in the Black Forest fire and are in Hawaii specifically to process and pray. Frankly, I've not been interested in buying anything, as we don't know what our living situation will be yet and I feel so emotionally low at times. But I'm so excited (for the first time in months) by your email, that I just made my first important "housing" decision—no matter our living situation, your piece will occupy a prominent place as a lasting reminder of a special time when our lives began finally to turn around. I cannot begin to tell you how much you've blessed us today—thanks, Brian.

On Sep 2, 2013, at 3:14 PM, Brian wrote:

Wow, John,

I'm not sure what to say. OK, I'm very sorry to hear about your house. When I heard about the fires, my thoughts and prayers were with those in the danger zone. I hope everyone you know from the area is alive and well. I'm glad you guys were able to make it to one of the most healing places in the world! I saw a certain light inside you that made me really want to find what you were looking for when you stopped by my little booth. I do what I do hoping that others recognize that same light inside of me, and I appreciate you very much for that. Thank you! Will you be returning to Colorado or have you found a new home among us here in the islands?

ALOHA!

On Sep 2, 2013, at 4:18 PM, I wrote:

OK—it's got to be the 30x30. And I'll hang it in a prominent place in our new home (which will likely be in Colorado Springs for now). Would very much appreciate it being numbered #1 with your signature and a note crediting its inspiration to me—if you're comfortable with that; it would mean a great deal to me.

On Sep 2, 2013, at 6:07 PM, Brian wrote:

You've got it John, thank you for the inspiration! Talk to you soon.

On Sep 16, 2013, at 4:21 PM, Brian wrote:

Hi John,

It seems like this order took forever! Sorry about that. I've decided to call the image "New Beginnings". It should be getting on the road now. Hope all is well with you.

Aloha

On Sep 16, 2013, at 4:06 PM, I wrote:

BTW, be honest with me—is it stunning gorgeous???

On Sep 16, 2013, at 9:06 PM, Brian wrote:

I have a print of it hanging in my hallway at home :-)

On Sep 18, 2013, at 11:02 AM, I wrote:

Wow, wow, wow!!! It's terrific—thank you, Brian.

On Sep 18, 2013, at 3:50 PM, Brian wrote:

Oh good, I'm so glad you like it! Let me know the next time you come to the island and I'll let you know if we make it to Colorado. Hope everything is going well with getting your new home in order. Keep in touch!

Aloha

I marvel at that beautiful picture many times every day, as it now sits in the entryway of our home, and I know that Brian talks frequently about the circumstances leading up to its capture. I have no doubt that God placed Brian in our lives at just the right time for just the right purpose.

The Piano Aficionado

We lost seven pianos in the fire, four of which were Steinways. Not that any of them was particularly valuable—they were all quite old and in various states of disrepair. You see, at one time I thought I might like to become a piano tuner-technician, so I began to collect restorable pianos. I had as many as twelve of them at one time, but on realizing that piano tuning wasn't for me, I gave several of them away, keeping the seven that would end up being destroyed in 2013.

Actually there was another piano that wasn't destroyed—a Steinway spinet that I'd given to my son Nate so he'd have a piano to play in his home. Nate's a truly gifted pianist, guitarist, and vocalist. This piano has an amazing story.

Quite a few years ago, I noticed it for sale in the classified ads of the local newspaper with an asking price of $400. Naturally I went to see it, and it surprised me. After all, it was green, made out of particle board, fairly beat up, with a Steinway fallboard decal.

Of course, I figured it couldn't be a real Steinway. *Aha,* I thought—the marking on the cast-iron plate wouldn't lie. I opened the top, and there it was: "Steinway & Sons." Still confused, I paid the seller and moved it to my home.

I found a book at the local library entitled *People and Pianos* by Theodore T. Steinway. It's a history of the famous Steinway family. Near the center of the book, in the World War II section, I saw a picture of a spinet with about fifteen Army soldiers in pith helmets crowded around a small piano, playing and singing.

The picture was strikingly similar to my piano! The caption read, "The G.I. Field Piano. Over 2,500 have been built since 1942." This piano was nothing less than a piece of history.

Here comes the fascinating part. Nate now had the only piano I'd previously owned. When he and his family decided to move to Plano, Texas, he didn't want to move the piano and said he'd like for me to have it back. So it sits in my home, having survived only through my generosity to my son and his reciprocal generosity to me. In the meantime, Nancy showed me an ad from the paper for a piano sale at a local warehouse. This is an annual event in Colorado Springs in which many pianos from local colleges and universities are offered at attractive prices when the schools are upgrading their current instruments.

As I entered the warehouse, a man approached me, asking me what I might be looking for. I told him my story about losing a number of nice pianos in a fire and that my wife had made me aware of the sale. He paused for a moment and said, "Sir, I have your piano right over here." He led me to a beautiful 6½ foot-long glossy grand piano with the lid removed.

He explained that this was a Bosendorfer, one of the finest pianos available, handmade in Austria. He boasted of its amazing action and sweet sustainable tones that were unmatched by other instruments. My heart leapt within my chest and we negotiated a price. The only downside was that the lid had sustained some damage in a recording studio and needed repair before I could take delivery.

A few weeks later, I decided to visit the piano, excited to learn when it would be delivered. The warehouse was noticeably empty with the exception of an elderly gentleman wearing a flat, duckbill cap, sitting at my piano. He was holding his cell phone over the strings and playing notes into the phone. I stood there awhile, observing him and wondering what he was doing. It turned out he was sampling the piano sounds for his wife on the other end. He didn't see me, and soon I went to the shop in back to talk with the technician.

When I reemerged into the showroom, the man was now playing a beautiful melody on my piano. I stood there observing, appreciating the incredible sounds coming forth. After some time he noticed me watching him and asked, "Sir, do you know what kind of piano this is? It's a Bosendorfer, the best made anywhere."

I told him I was aware that it was a Bosendorfer, to which he responded, "But are you aware of how magnificent it truly is? It's made by hand; Bosendorfer makes only 200 pianos a year; just look at how magnificent it is!" He motioned for me to follow him to another piano located nearby. He sat at a nine-foot-long Steinway Model D concert grand and played another melody. Then he led me back to the Bosendorfer where he played the same melody. He paused, then asked, "Can you tell the difference?"

"Of course," I honestly replied. I couldn't remain silent anymore. "Sir, are you aware that *I* bought this piano?"

He stood. "So *you're* the doctor who bought it!" He obviously knew all about me. "Do you have any idea what a remarkable instrument you've purchased? This piano is brand new."

I assured him it wasn't brand new—just in like-new condition.

He introduced himself as Harvey E. S. Karlsen, an ordained minister who operated InterFACE Ministries, helping international students, immigrants, and refugees since 1972. Besides this ministry, he had a deep appreciation for fine pianos, having a Petrov (of Czech origin) of his own. We talked for an hour and a half, during which he learned of the book I was working on, asking numerous questions and indicating he'd like a copy. He was fascinated and asked if I had another hour or two so he could take me to lunch and we could talk more. Sadly I had to decline, but we agreed to meet again.

What an interesting visit and discussion with someone I certainly hadn't expected to meet. After all, my plan was to visit with the warehouse owner, who wasn't there that day. It clearly turned out to have been God's plan that I meet Harvey Karlsen, a minister who was off the world's radar screen. I couldn't have orchestrated this important meeting had I tried.

One doesn't have to think very hard to recall the many divine appointments God has set up for us. Isn't it amazing how He works in willing vessels, shattering our own plans and installing His own?

A Man Named Ed Mason

My last tour in the Air Force was at Hanscom AFB near Boston, where I served as military commander of the Air

Force Geophysics Laboratory, a facility developing many interesting space technologies. Nancy and I attended a good-sized Assembly of God church called Mount Hope Christian Center in Burlington, Massachusetts. It was there that I met Ed Mason, an eighty-year-old former welder who helped build many of the bridges in the Boston area. Ed led the men's ministry when we first arrived, and I'll never forget a powerful lesson he taught on *rust*, entitled "Rust Never Sleeps." He was drawing from his welding background where he learned that if you paint over steel that has rust within, the rust will continue to oxidize and eventually find its way out, even if you do a good job with the paint. The analogy he was drawing, of course, was that we cannot bury secret sin for long—it will eventually come out. "Sin never sleeps," Ed would say, and that particular lesson has had a profound impact on me.

Ed and I became best friends, sharing breakfast just about every week. He sported a big scruffy beard, and on asking him how he was doing, he'd always answer, "I'm bright-eyed and bushy faced!" We shared many of the same interests, including our love of eagles and of Christian music (particularly from the Gaither Vocal Band). One thing we didn't have in common was that Ed raised birds, or "boids," as he would call them, having over two hundred at one time—ducks, geese, pigeons, and peacocks, to name a few. One day I asked him if he ever ate his birds.

"Just once," he replied. He said he served up one of his ducks for dinner one evening. On staring at it, his daughter Valerie became pale and upset, then screamed, "Dad, that's Howard!" How was Ed to know he'd inadvertently selected her pet duck?

The thing I most appreciated about Ed was his forthrightness about his relationship with Christ. Everyone who hung around him for any length of time *knew* without question what was most important to him. He was as much like Paul the apostle as anyone I knew. Paul—and Ed—may not have pleased everyone they met with what they shared, but no one could possibly misunderstand their boldly proclaimed message. I simply loved Ed for his candor and drive, and counted myself privileged to know him.

Ed died Sunday, January 5, 2014. I found out when I received a telephone call from his senior pastor, and learned that Ed requested that I speak at his funeral. Unfortunately I couldn't do so on such short notice, so I wrote the following piece which was read publicly:

> I considered Ed Mason to be my best friend while I lived in Boston, first while in the Air Force, then as a student in optometry school, and I feel blessed to have been able to spend so much time with him. During the time since we moved to Colorado Springs in late 2000, Ed and I talked and reminisced over the telephone regularly.
>
> There are two things that stand out about this incredible man as I recall the sweetness of his life:
>
> 1. He loved the Lord unlike any other I've ever known; it was impossible for one to be around him very long without knowing what the most important thing in his life was—his relationship with the Lord Jesus. He was the consummate "fisherman," always looking for ways to "haul in" a new catch for the "Master Fisherman."
>
> 2. He was competitive—in a fun way. For some time each of us tried to outdo the other by wearing a new eagle tie to church each week, always commenting on the other's tie; you see, we both loved eagles, one of our favorite Scripture verses being Isaiah 40:31. One day I thought I'd

fix him—I wore a Save-the-Children tie with crudely drawn turkeys on it that were created by a six-year-old named David. When Ed saw me in the lobby of the church, he exclaimed (in a loud voice), "What a sick looking boid, Rabins!" I said, "Why don't you embarrass me more and repeat that even louder, Ed?" He *did*, remarking, "I said what a sick looking boid, Rabins!" I then took the tie off, presented it to him as a gift, and asked him to read what I'd written on the back, loud enough so everyone could hear it. By this time many had gathered to listen to the exchange. He then read the following aloud: "This tie is dedicated to my faithful prayer partner, Ed Mason. What a privilege and honor it is to wear his likeness throughout the day!" Everyone present laughed for a long time, but no one laughed harder or longer than did Ed.

Ed taught me so much about what life is really all about. I miss him more than I can express in words, but know that heaven is richer today because of his incredible smile, wit, and love.

One of the men who was part of the men's ministry remembered Ed in a similar way:

My condolences to the family of Edward A. Mason.

I met Ed at the Assemblies of God in Burlington, MA many years ago. I would say Ed was a man's man. As an iron worker, he built bridges for us to cross. As a man's man, and a man who loved God and those around him, he built relational bridges that allowed men to know and love God and one another. His laugh always made me smile, and his wisdom came from a life full of God's Word. He led a men's group at church that was called Bridge Builders. He would show up wearing his blue work clothes and tell us life stories, and how bridges work. Ed was an inspiration to me.

I always tell folks about this great man I knew, and will always do my best to retell his stories. Ed was a man after God's own heart. He was a good friend. I will miss you, Ed.

Mark Mulvaney,

Wilmington, Massachusetts

Obviously I'm not the only one to have felt this way about this incredible saint.

Have you had an Ed Mason in your life? Do you have one now? If so, relish every moment; if you don't have one, then look for one.

Incidentally, Ed gave the turkey tie back to me when I left Boston, wanting me to keep it. As I mentioned earlier, I've truly missed only a small fraction of my possessions destroyed by the fire. This tie was certainly one of those I miss most.

I'll conclude this chapter with a quiz I received from a dear friend. It's a piece that has been widely attributed to Charles Schulz, the creator of the Peanuts comic strip, although the Charles Schulz Museum denies it as having come from him. *Who* wrote it isn't nearly as important as the wisdom it contains:

Charles Schulz Philosophy

You don't have to actually answer the questions. Just read straight through, and you'll get the point.

1. Name the five wealthiest people in the world.

2. Name the last five Heisman trophy winners.

3. Name the last five winners of the Miss America.

4. Name ten people who have won the Nobel or Pulitzer Prize.

5. Name the last half dozen Academy Award winners for best actor and actress.

6. Name the last decade's worth of World Series winners.

How did you do?

The point is, none of us remember the headliners of yesterday. These are no second-rate achievers. They're the best in their fields. But the applause dies. Awards tarnish. Achievements are forgotten. Accolades and certificates are buried with their owners.

Here's another quiz. See how you do on this one:

1. List a few teachers who aided your journey through school.

2. Name three friends who've helped you through a difficult time.

3. Name five people who've taught you something worthwhile.

4. Think of a few people who've made you feel appreciated and special.

5. Think of five people you enjoy spending time with.

Easier?

The lesson: The people who make a difference in your life are not the ones with the most credentials, the most money, or the most awards. They're the ones who care.

"Don't worry about the world coming to an end today. It's already tomorrow in Australia." (Charles Schulz)

What I Need to Let Go of:

Having a Best Friend Other Than God

Most of us had a best friend while growing up, perhaps more than one. It's wonderful being able to count on another who would do anything for us. It's such a good feeling to know that someone else values us as a best friend. While it seems impossible to me, some claim to have more than one best friend at a time. I don't get that, but I've heard it said. Regardless, a true best friend represents the closest thing to unconditional love that we have in another human being.

The problem is that even best friends will let us down at times, and that can be discouraging, especially if our expectations are high. Being let down by my best friend, let alone a good friend, makes me wonder if I can count on anyone to be consistently there for me. I've discovered that truly there's no one who can meet that expectation—except the Lord Jesus, the *only* One who gives complete, unconditional love. He *never* fails me, He *never* lets me down, and He loves me no matter what!

Let me restate an astounding truth: God is the only One who can honestly say, "John, I love you exactly the way you are, and I love you too much to leave you there."

It has taken me a long time to appreciate that revelation, but here's what's wonderful about doing so: I become better at understanding and forgiving when a good friend lets me down, and I'm therefore able to help him grow in both giving and receiving unconditional love. It's a beautiful thing!

As trite as this may sound, God is my best friend. Whenever I begin to think that another person is my best friend, I must check that thought at the door and ensure that I'm giving God His rightful place.

Application Questions about Who We Know

1. Who's the most famous person you've ever met? How did you feel being able to talk with this person? Did he or she call you by your name? If so, how did that make you feel? Would that person remember you today?

2. Do you find yourself seeking opportunities to meet "important" people? Why do you think you do this?

3. Now think of an instance where God used you to touch someone else, someone who wasn't famous. Recount all the details surrounding this event. How did it make you feel? Would that person remember you today?

4. Why do we seek affirmation from others when, in fact, the King of the universe loves us unconditionally?

5. Psalm 46:10 directs us to be still and know that He is God. Do you have trouble doing this? Do you have trouble carving out time from your busy day to simply sit and wait upon God? Does your to-do list take

priority? Are you perhaps reluctant to be still and listen to what God might tell you? Are you more comfortable being around other people than around God?

6. Who was your favorite teacher in school? What made this person so special to you? How has this teacher's influence impacted your most important life decisions? Has God placed an "Ed Mason" in your life? What was this person like and how did that impact you?

7. Do you *really* believe that God, who knows you best, loves you *exactly as you are*, even in the midst of your sin and dark areas, in spite of the parts of you that you may be ashamed of?

The Seven Defining Truths
Distilled

The Bottom Line

*For to me, to live is Christ
and to die is gain.*
Philippians 1:21

Paul goes on in the first chapter of Philippians to say this:

> I am torn between the two: I desire to depart and be with Christ, which is better by far; but it is more necessary for you that I remain in the body. Convinced of this, I know that I will remain, and I will continue with all of you for your progress and joy in the faith, so that through my being with you again your boasting in Christ Jesus will abound on account of me. (Philippians 1:24-26)

Clearly Paul had the right eternal perspective. He knew his purpose and destiny. There was no question in his mind what he was about.

When I was a new Christian with great passion but no depth of understanding for my newfound faith, I had little excitement about the Lord's imminent return. Life was good, I thought, and I wasn't ready to give up a great career, home, family, and friends. "Lord, you know that I love you," I'd find myself saying, "but I'm not ready to give up what I have just now."

I don't feel that way so much anymore, and my attitude has been changing toward a more eternal perspective. Apparently it took a fire to kick me in the seat of my pants.

What We Learn from Sand Crabs

During our second trip to Hawaii following the fire, Nancy and I did far less structured activity and instead spent lots of time sitting on the beach—processing, praying, planning, and dreaming.

One morning we were watching the sunrise, appreciating that we were all alone on the beach. There were no other people around, but we *weren't* alone. After a while, Nancy looked down to her left and noticed a fairly good-sized sand crab digging a hole next to her. When she called it to my attention, the crab quickly scurried down the hole he'd just dug. Then I noticed another crab to my right doing the same thing. He seemed to be waiting for me to glance in his direction, after which he also ran down the hole he'd dug. We began to more carefully survey the beach around us and were astonished at how many crabs were running here and there. There must have been hundreds. Everywhere we looked, there they were.

Here's what's interesting: they didn't come onto the scene suddenly—they were there all along. We just hadn't noticed before. It made me ask what else I might be missing simply because I'm not looking for it.

What an incredible life lesson this turned out to be! Nancy's favorite Scripture verse has always been this one:

Be still and know that I am God. (Psalm 46:10)

It's beginning to become mine as well. Here's why: we miss so much going on around us because we fail to look for it. We're so busy with our to-do lists, pressures at work and home, anxieties about a myriad of things, getting everything done that we determine needs doing, that we miss some of the most important things God has for us.

How many opportunities have we missed—because we weren't looking for them—to share the light inside us with others who are hurting?

If we would only devote time to waiting on God and asking Him for direction, He'd speak to us, not necessarily in words, but by the Holy Spirit's unction. When I devote time to doing this and eagerly seek Him at the start of a day, I'm always amazed at how many opportunities for doing God's business manage to "pop up." It's not a coincidence. God has designed us to rely on Him, and to be connected to Him in an intimate way. The more I engage Him in this way, the more sense it makes. I'm learning to speak less to Him, and to listen more. It's really that simple.

Lessons from Job

Job lost everything—his children, his property, most of his friends, and his health. In spite of these formidable tragedies, Job did the right thing, simply because it was the right thing—keeping his faith strong and never wavering in his relationship with God. He knew he'd be rewarded in the end. And of course he was, as seen in the final chapter of his namesake book:

> After Job had prayed for his friends, the LORD made him prosperous again and gave him twice as much as he had before…. The LORD blessed the latter part of Job's life more than the first. He had fourteen thousand sheep, six thousand camels, a thousand yoke of oxen, and a thousand donkeys. And he also had seven sons and three daughters. (42:10-13).

Job knew the right thing to do and *did* it, because he knew it was worth the price.

It's Worth the Price

Earlier in this book I quoted a friend who said that our anxiety comes from wanting a future outcome over which we have no control. I mentioned how she challenged me with a question: "What do you need to let go of in order to live in the present with joyfulness?"

Her question floored me, and as I pondered it, I realized it was probably the most important one ever asked of me. Working on the answers to it has probably made the biggest difference in my life to date.

Here are the best answers I've come up with thus far. You'll recall that each one capped one of the seven defining-truth chapters.

> *What I need to let go of in order to live in the present,*
> *with joyfulness:*

1. The fear that joy is somehow outside my reach *(what I own)*.

2. Viewing myself as a human "doing" versus a human "being" *(what I've done)*.

3. Fear of being alone *(my tragedies)*.

4. Entertaining (dwelling on) below-the-line thinking *(what I think)*.

5. Feelings of rejection *(what others think)*.

6. Addictive behaviors and thought patterns with accompanying unrealistic, fantasy-laden dreams

whereby I control the future and attach to the outcome *(what I control)*.

7. Having a best friend, other than God *(who I know)*.

Again, there are seven items on the list. Each of these items has aligned itself quite nicely with one of the seven defining truths contained in this book (listed in parentheses). What's most fascinating to me, however, is that each one of these represents an area that God is working on in my life *right now*.

As I let them go, I'm learning to replace each of them with something else:

1. The knowledge that there's incredible joy in Him—and, truly, *only* in Him.

2. Viewing myself as a human "being" versus a human "doing."

3. The confidence that even when no one else is near, I'm never alone.

4. Dwelling on upright, wholesome thoughts (as we're commanded to do in Philippians 4:8).

5. Feelings of acceptance, love, and value.

6. Genuine faith that wholly trusts in Him.

7. Having a best friend who is, in fact, God.

As I began this book with my testimony of coming to faith, it's as though the remainder of the book is essentially my autobiography since that point. It represents all the steps God is using in my healing process toward maturation.

Here's what's cool: when I demonstrate the willingness to release the former seven things and allow God to do His work, I experience lots of the pain, negative thoughts, and difficult emotions that formerly drove me into my addictive behaviors. But there's a big difference now. Now I choose not to go there, but instead to face the pain maturely, with an expectation that God will use it productively to grow me up.

And I find He does just that. When I make right choices, the pain lasts only a short time. But the reward—my growth—lasts forever.

I absolutely love where I am—right now!

And while we're on the subject of becoming willing to let things go, consider the following devotional:

"Get Rid of Some Stuff"—May 7, 2015 (from *Living in the Spirit Meditations* by Louise Manigault)

Sometimes you look through the newspaper or on the internet and see some furniture that you would like to purchase for your home. You can imagine how great it will look and how much you will enjoy it. You're almost set to buy it, but then you stop and think, "I have to get rid of this old, outdated stuff first." You hesitate because you used to like the old furniture, and it served a purpose through the years. You have to make a decision. You can either stay with the old stuff or move it out in order to bring in the new stuff.

The same thing happens with your spiritual life. God always has something new for you.

His plan will bring you peace and fulfillment, but you have to get rid of some stuff that has been blocking the flow of God's blessings. It could be friends, work or, unfortunately, a family member. It could be adverse situations that you have been living with and tolerating even though, deep down, you are miserable. It could also be your emotional state of mind and the false belief that you are not worthy of God's blessings.

"Blessed are those you choose and bring near to live in your courts!" (Psalm 65:4).

"How great is your goodness, which you have stored up for those who fear you, which you bestow in the sight of those who take refuge in you." (Psalm 31:19).

God is waiting to bless you, but you have to get rid of some stuff to make room for all that God has planned for you.

Blessings,

Louise Manigault.

And how about this quote by Louise Smith: "You can't reach for anything new if your hands are still full of yesterday's junk."

I don't believe I could have said it any better—how about you?

The Bottom Line

If we find ourselves drawing our value from what we own or from what we've done; if we feel special because of our tragedies; if our worth derives from what we think or what others think; or if our sense of importance comes from what we think we control or from whom we know; then we must reconsider. God doesn't really care about any of that—He just cares about us!

It seems at times that the road we're traveling is hot and tiring. We often think about giving up, wondering if it's worth it. That's when God reminds us that He's always with us and *never* gives up on us:

> And surely I am with you always, to the very end of the age. (Matthew 28:20)

He also lets us know that we need never operate in our own power:

> For my yoke is easy and my burden is light. (Matthew 11:30)

I recently participated in a retreat at a lovely monastery in Sedalia, Colorado. One morning I was heading out of my room to walk along some of the magnificent hiking paths there. Just outside my door I felt a "nudge" to go back in and grab some notepaper. Going back into the room, I convinced myself that if I received anything worth writing down, I'd just remember it when I returned back to my room. I headed out a second time, empty-handed. Then that same nudge convinced me to reenter the room and grab the notepad.

At the end of a brisk, refreshing hike, I sat down to think and pray. The Lord gave me much to write down, not the least of which was this:

In *me* there is *nothing* of value.

In *Christ* is *everything.*

The value in me is the Christ in me.

Later, on the ride back from the retreat, I heard a new song—a song that positively moved me. It's entitled *When All That's Left Is to Believe* and is performed by Clay Crosse. It exquisitely embodies the bottom line of this book. The more I listened to it, the more appropriate it seemed to include its chorus here:

> When all that's left is to believe,
> I give my doubts and fears to You
> And fall down on my knees.
> I may not have the answers now,
> But You give me what I need.
> So Father I will cling to You
> When all that's left is to believe.

> My soul finds rest in God alone; my salvation comes from Him. He alone is my rock and my salvation; He is my fortress, I will never be shaken. (Psalm 62:1-2)

Jimmy Dodd, president of PastorServe, once preached these words from the pulpit: "When God is all you have, you realize that God is all you need."

Corrie ten Boom, a Christian whose family saved some eight hundred Jewish lives during the Holocaust, expressed the same thought a bit differently: "You can never learn that Christ is all you need, until Christ is all you have."

Reworded again, this is precisely the bottom line, the essence of *all* the lessons I'm learning through tragedy:

When we come to understand that
all we truly have is Jesus,
we discover the joyous truth that…